CASE STUDIES IN
CULTURAL ANTHROPOLOGY

GENERAL EDITORS

George and Louise Spindler

STANFORD UNIVERSITY

The Igbo of Southeast Nigeria

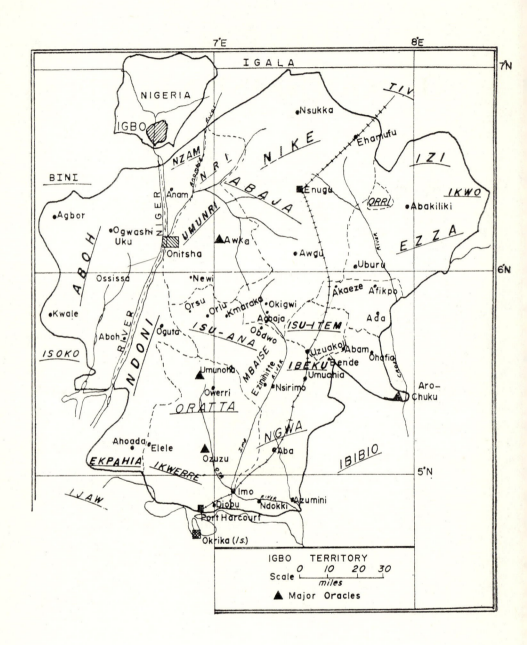

IGBO TERRITORY
Scale 0 10 20 30
miles
▲ Major Oracles

THE IGBO
OF SOUTHEAST NIGERIA

By

VICTOR C. UCHENDU
Northwestern University

HOLT, RINEHART AND WINSTON

NEW YORK   CHICAGO   SAN FRANCISCO   TORONTO   LONDON

Foreword

About the Series

These case studies in cultural anthropology are designed to bring to students in the social sciences insights into the richness and complexity of human life as it is lived in different ways and in different places. They are written by men and women who have lived in the societies they write about, and who are professionally trained as observers and interpreters of human behavior. The authors are also teachers, and in writing their books they have kept the students who will read them foremost in their minds. It is our belief that when an understanding of ways of life very different from one's own is gained, abstractions and generalizations about social structure, cultural values, subsistence techniques, and the other universal categories of human social behavior become meaningful.

About the Author

Victor Chikezie Uchendu is a candidate for the doctorate in anthropology at Northwestern University. A graduate of the University of Ibadan, Nigeria, he received his Bachelor of Science (Honors) degree from London University. At Ibadan, Mr. Uchendu distinguished himself by winning the Departmental Prize (1959–1960) and the Faculty Prize (1960–1961) of the Department of Economics and Social Studies. He has carried out research among the southeastern Igbo, his home area. He has also completed a field study of the migratory labor patterns of the Navaho Indians (1964–1965). His articles on aspects of Igbo culture have been published in academic journals.

About the Book

This case study is one of those rare events in anthropological literature—an ethnography written by one of the people whose culture is being described. Written by an Igbo about his own people, this case study penetrates to the heart of the Igbo culture and social system. Mr. Uchendu shows us how the people in this Nigerian society think about the world around them, and how they conceive of their own social system and its workings. Descriptions of the thinking and feeling of a people from the inside are not frequent in anthropological literature, for it is difficult for the observer from the outside world to penetrate beyond manifest behavior to the inner patterns of a way of life. The author has also given us an intellectually satisfying analysis of the objective workings of the Igbo system. We come to an understanding of how the Igbo make a living, how they govern themselves, how the family is founded, how the network of kinship functions, as well as many other dimensions of Igbo life. And finally he shows us how the Igbo have responded to contact with European culture.

GEORGE AND LOUISE SPINDLER
General Editors

Stanford, California
August 1965

Acknowledgment

I wish to express my indebtedness to Professor Paul Bohannan, my adviser at Northwestern University, who not only encouraged this study but recommended it to the editors of this series; to Mr. Robert C. Mitchell, Department of Sociology, Northwestern University, who read the first few chapters and offered many useful suggestions; and to the Rockefeller Foundation, whose scholarship made my graduate training in anthropology possible.

Contents

Foreword   vii

Introduction   1

1. The Igbo World   11
The World of Man and the World of Spirits, 11
Maintaining Cosmological Balance, 12
Manipulating His World, 15
Cyclical Nature of Status Seeking, 16
Transparent Living, 17
"A Country Is Spoiled by Men," 18
A World of Change, 19
Equalitarianism, 19
Summary, 20

2. How the Igbo Make Their Living   22
Farming: Land Tenure, 22
The Farming Cycle, 24
The Preparation of Palm Oil, 26
Trading, 27
The Marketplace and the "Market Peace," 28
The "Market Ring," 28
Price Determination, 29
Livestock Tenancy, 30
Wage Labor, 31

3. Helping the Town "To Get Up"   34
Earlier Patterns of "Getting Up," 34
Modern Development and Self-Help, 36
"Human Investment," 36
The Improvement Unions, 37

4. Igbo Ways in Government   39
Authority in the "Family," 39
Autonomy of the Village, 41
Government of the Village-Group (Town), 44
Three Sample Governments, 44

Igboland under Colonial Rule, 46
  The Direct Administration, 46
  The Warrant Chiefs, 46
  The Reforms of 1930–1931, 48
Changes Preceding Independence, 48

5. Founding a New Family   49

Emphasis on Married Status, 49
Types of Marriage, 50
Stages in the Marriage Process, 51
The Adjustment of the New Bride, 53
The "Big Compound" Ideal of the Igbo Family, 54
The Developmental Cycle of the "Big Compound," 55
New Trends in the Igbo Family System, 56

6. Growing Up in an Igbo Village   57

Igbo Ideas about Conception, 57
A Child Is Born, 58
The Umbilical Cord, 58
A Child Is Named, 60
"Churching"—An Outing Ceremony, 60
The Igbo Child Shares Two Worlds, 61

7. The Kinship Network   64

The Agnates, 64
The Mother's Agnates, 66
The "Remote" Kinsmen, 67
Balancing Kinship Conflicts, 67
Naming the Kin, 68

8. Igbo Hospitality   71

Principles of Hospitality, 71
Forms of Hospitality, 72
"Kola" Hospitality, 74

9. Nonkinship Associations   76

Work Groups, 76
Credit Associations, 77
Dibia Associations, 81
Title Societies, 82
Associations and Village Integration, 82

10. Status Placement among Igbo　84

Age and Kinship Status, 84
Marriage and Social Position, 86
The Status of Women, 86
Diala and Non-Diala Status, 87
The Osu System of Slavery, 89
Leadership and Status Placement, 90
Associational Status, 91
Western Impact on the Igbo Status System, 92

11. Igbo Gods and Oracles　94

Igbo Ideas of the High God, 94
Ala, the Earth-Goddess, 95
Other Spirits, 96
Igbo Oracles, 100
The Ancestors, 102

12. The Igbo and Culture Contact　103

Orthography　107

References　109

Recommended Reading　111

Disgwu, a solo dancer, entertains at a "second burial" ceremony in an Igbo village.

Processing palm oil by the traditional method, showing the first stage in the "soft" oil production.

Igbo women celebrate a gala day.

Ɔba, *an Igbo yam house.*

Left: A cement tomb sculpture: a new symbol of status for a deceased Igbo chief.

The Igbo of Southeast Nigeria

Introduction

THIS BOOK introduces the reader to the Igbo-speaking people of Nigeria. Located in southeastern Nigeria between latitude 5 to 7 degrees north and longitude 6 to 8 degrees east, they occupy an area of some 15,800 square miles. Before it enters the Atlantic Ocean through a network of distributaries which characterize its delta, the Niger River divides the Igbo country into two unequal parts. The greater portion lies in what is now called the Eastern Region of Nigeria, while a smaller triangular portion, west of the Niger, is part of Nigeria's fourth—the Midwestern Region.

The western Igbo are territorially marked off from the Bini and Warri, their non-Igbo neighbors. On the left bank of the Niger, the eastern Igbo stretch from the Niger Delta, where the Ijaw and Ogoni are their southern neighbors, to the north, where the Igala and the Tiv mark the boundary. On the eastern boundary are the Yako and the Ibibio. Though separated by the Niger and thus falling into two separate political units, the western and eastern Igbo have retained their cultural as well as their psychic unity. In modern times their attitude toward political questions and their identification with what they regard as their own "leaders" reveal the solidarity between the Igbo peoples on both sides of the Niger.

The Igbo country exhibits a wide variety of physical features. The Niger River contributes to this diversity. The most important rivers—Niger, Imo, Anambra, and Urasi—flow from north to south thus indicating a steep northward gradient. Four distinct areas may be distinguished: the riverine, the delta, the central, and the northeastern belts. The riverine and the delta belts are served by the Niger and its tributaries; they are low lying, are heavily inundated during the rainy season, and are very fertile. The headwaters of the Imo and Urasi rivers serve the central belt, a relatively high plain which gradually fades into the Okigwi-Awgu plateau. Although the Cross River does not flow through most southeastern Igbo regions, it helps to drain the Afikpo and Ikwo areas. The Udi highlands, which contain coal deposits, comprise the only coal-mining area in West Africa. The modern city of Enugu is a coal-mining city as well as the administrative capital for Eastern Nigeria.

Igboland has a tropical climate. The average annual temperature is about 80° F., with an annual range of between 5° and 10°. The rainy and dry seasons are well marked. The former begins in April and lasts to October, when the

1

dry season commences. Rainfall is heavier in the south than in the north, many areas having more than 70 inches a year. During the rainy season a "break" occurs in August. Southeasterners call it ɔkɔchi ji okoᵌ—the drought favorable to the growth of ji oko (yam). Important in the seasonal cycle are the southwest monsoon winds that bring rain and the northeast winds that are dry and dusty as well as cold. These winds, as well as the dry, dusty chilly conditions they cause, are locally known as ɵgere—harmattan. They are the farmer's friend. They open the bush, dry the clearings, kill some of the insects which destroy crops and make the burning of rubbish easy.

In many parts of northern and central Igbo country today, the big forests have become secondary bush or eroded gullies. The former is caused by the pattern of farming known as "bush fallowing,"[2] while the latter results from rain water sweeping down from steep slopes across cultivated farm lands which had little surface vegetation to check it. Oil palm (Elaeis guineensis) and raphia palm (Raphia vinifera), our most important economic assets, either are growing wild or are cultivated in plantations. Hardwood trees such as obeche, ɔji (iroko), ɵkɵ, and ɛdo provide timber. Indiscriminate slaughter of animals in a country where tsetse flies limit the type and number that can survive, a slaughter hastened by the early introduction of flintlock guns, accounts for the scarcity of game. However, ivory horns and ivory ornaments which are features of ceremonials tell a history of a glorious past rich in elephants.

According to Nigeria's census of 1953, the Igbo-speaking people numbered five and a half million. This population is very unevenly distributed, the bulk of it concentrated in a geographical axis formed by Onitsha, Orlu, Okigwi, and Mbaise areas. Along the Onitsha-Mbaise axis the density of population exceeds 1000 per square mile in many places thus giving us one of the world's most densely populated rural areas subsisting on root crops raised through hoe culture. In all directions from this "population" axis, the density of population falls below the Igbo average of 350 per square mile but remains well above Nigeria's average of 85 per square mile.

When and from where the Igbo came into their present territory is not known. Their origin is a subject of much speculation. The people have no common tradition of origin. It is only rather recently that some Igbo-speaking communities have ceased to claim that they are not Igbo. What local traditions the Igbo have do not provide clues to their origin. It is for this reason that some Western writers on the colonial era treated the Igbo as "a people without history." We have since come to know better. A people with a culture are a people with some form of history. The Igbo have a culture; they have also a history—an unwritten history which it is the task of the culture historian to piece together. The Igbo culture historian is presently handicapped because there is little ar-

---

[1] A guide to the sounds represented by the phonetic symbols will be found on page 107.

[2] Bush fallowing erroneously termed "shifting cultivation" is a method of farming in which a farmer leaves a piece of land after cultivation for a period of years (ranging from two to eight, depending on the pressure on land) and returns to it after it has regained its fertility through natural regeneration of vegetation.

cheological data from which he can draw. His only sources of data are cultural: fragmentary oral traditions and the correlation of cultural traits.

An analysis of demographic patterns, trait lists, and other cultural features, combined with available local traditions, leads us to two interrelated hypotheses of Igbo origin: that there exists a core area which may be called the "nuclear" Igboland; and that waves of immigrant communities from the north and the west planted themselves on the border of the nuclear Igboland as early as the fourteenth or the fifteenth century.

The belt formed by Owerri, Awka, Orlu, and Okigwi divisions constitutes this "nuclear" area: its people have no tradition of coming from any other place. It is a most densely populated area. We assume an early migration from this area into the Nsukka-Udi highlands in the north and into Ikwerri, Etche, Asa, and Ndokki in the south. The eastern Isuama claim to have come from this center. Ngwa traditions point to their secondary migration from Mbaise. The general character of the secondary and tertiary dispersion of population in the recent past tended to be short and in all directions: north, south, east, and west. This was a movement that tended to homogenize Igbo culture. The main attractions for dispersion included an ever-widening frontier of the "no man's land" and the desire to found independent villages, but the most compelling reasons were the pressure of population in certain areas and natural disasters that made continued settlement in some places inauspicious.

In addition to this pattern of migration from the nuclear area, there are traditions, confirmed by intrusive culture traits, of peoples who entered Igbo territory in about the fourteenth or the fifteenth century. Of these, there are the Nri, in whom Igala influence is marked; and the Nzam and Anam, who combine Bini and Igala traits. Onitsha, Oguta, and the Ezechima group of villages in western Igbo claim affinity with Bini and have their kingship institution to show "as evidence of descent." Their eponymous ancestor Chima—an Igbo name— conclusively demonstrates that these Ezechima people were not Bini but Igbo-speaking people once under the political domination of Benin Kingdom. The distinguishing characteristics of these "late-comers" include their geographical marginality, kingship institution, hierarchical title system, and *amosu* tradition (witchcraft).

If the origin of the Igbo is uncertain, the word "Igbo" is not without its own puzzles. Until comparatively recent times, some Igbo-speaking peoples like the Onitsha, Nri, and Oguta claimed that they were not Igbo, and used the word as a term of abuse for their "less cultured" neighbors. Today, "Igbo" is used in three senses: to refer to Igbo territory, to the domestic speakers of the language, and to the language spoken by them. According to Greenberg's (1949:87) classification of African languages, the Igbo language is one of the speech communities in the Kwa subfamily of the Niger-Congo family. It is marked by a complicated system of tones used to distinguish meaning and grammatical relationships, a wide range of dialectical variations that is a source of difficulty to Westerners but not to the Igbo, and a tendency to vowel elision which makes it difficult to express a few of the spoken words in writing. If we follow a longitudinal dialectic profile, we encounter mutual intelligibility between the communities at the center and those at the poles; but between the polar communities intelligibility varies from partial to almost nil. These polar dialects are the result of greater marginal isolation rather than survivors of a previous dialect cradleland.

European contact with the Igbo-speaking peoples dates back to the arrival of the Portuguese in the middle of the fifteenth century. For nearly four centuries (1434–1807), the Niger Coast formed a "contact community"—the contact point between European and African traders: the Portuguese from the fifteenth and sixteenth centuries, the Dutch from the seventeenth, and the British from the eighteenth century. It was a period of trade on the coast rather than one of conquest or empire building in the hinterland. The chief item provided by the Igbo was slaves, many of whom came to the New World. The monopoly held by the coastal slavers (traders from the Niger states) reduced Igbo slavers to the role of middlemen who rarely dealt directly with European slavers. The local trade currencies of this period included manillas, copper rods, iron bars, whisky, and, later, cowrie shells.

With the abolition of the slave trade in 1807, a new trading epoch opened. There was a shift from the traffic in men to the traffic in the raw materials of industry: palm products, timber, elephant tusks, and spices became the merchandise of the "legitimate" trader. With this shift, the European traders could no longer be confined to the coast. They saw their real interest, the "trader's frontier," in the hinterland, which was still the source of both illegitimate and legitimate goods. In the struggle to establish a "free trade" hinterland between 1807–1885, the British companies played a decisive role for Britain through their joint program, which combined aggressive trading with aggressive imperialism.

When in 1900, the Protectorate of Southern Nigeria was created from the former British Niger Company's administrative area and the Niger Coast Protectorate, and control of this area passed from the British Foreign Office to the Colonial Office, Igboland had been technically treated as a British colony even before it was formally conquered and pacified. Between 1902, when the Aro "Long Juju" was destroyed, and 1914, when Northern and Southern Nigeria were amalgamated, there were twenty-one British military expeditions into Igboland. It was not until 1928, when Igbo men were made to pay tax for the first time in their history, that it became clear to them that they were a subject people.

No sketch of the British penetration of Igboland is complete without a word about the missionaries. It was in 1857 that Bishop Crowther successfully established a Church Missionary Society mission at Onitsha. The Roman Catholic Mission followed in 1885. Onitsha thus became the religious and educational center of these two great proselytizing missions as well as the base for British military penetration into northern Igboland. Although the missionaries enjoyed the protective power and the military prestige of the advancing colonial power, it was the "mystery of the written word"—the psychology of the "bush schools" founded by them—rather than military might or the "content of the Bible" which assured their success among the Igbo.

In the following chapters, the reader will be introduced to Igbo society and culture by one of its culture-bearers who has been privileged to gather his data as a "full participant" and tries to write as "a man of science." These two statements need a brief explanation, for the reader may like to know how I lived in a culture I am describing, and how objective I am in reporting it.

I was born during a period of great social change marked by a violent cultural protest. The depression of the late 1920s was having its impact on our economy. Palm oil and palm kernels, which had become our principal cash earner after European contact, could not find ready markets. Our people could not earn the money with which to buy machine-made goods. In the midst of this poverty, which we could not understand, a program of census taking and the property assessment of our women was launched by the Colonial Administration. This generated the rumor that the taxation of women was imminent, which sparked off the "Women's Riot," or, as our people choose to call it, the "Women's War." (For details, see Chapter 4.)

Though emotionally involved in the Women's War, which started in November 1929, my mother did not actually "go to war." Although other pregnant women "went to war," it was considered a particularly grave risk for my mother to participate: my mother was a divorcee and my father had married her in spite of the opposition of his family. This opposition was not due to the status of my mother as a divorcee; rather, it was due to a feeling that she might not bear children.

My mother comes from a big family. Her father, Ogbuishi ("Head Cutter"), had the largest compound[3] I have ever known. According to popular estimate, Ogbuishi had more than a hundred wives, but when I came to know him, he had about thirty. His unmarried sons exploited his great passion for marrying many wives. Cases are known to me, and I used to tease the girls concerned, of Ogbuishi's daughters who were introduced to him as prospective brides so that he would pay their bridewealth. It was in this way that some of his sons acquired money to pay bridewealth for their own wives. When he died in 1939, I played my role as *okɛnɛ* (daughter's child) during his first and second burial rites. In a "big family" like my mother's, it was impossible for a father to know all his children. The child-mother bond thus was a strong one, and half-sibling rivalry and co-wife competition were marked.

In my mother's youth, the Christian churches were preaching a radical doctrine. Challenging the Igbo practice of killing twins, they protected these infants. With the feverish enthusiasm of a convert, my mother carried in her arms twins who had been isolated in a hut outside the village limits. (Setting the twins apart was a concession to the Colonial Administration. Hitherto the fate of twins had been instant death.) The news that my mother, then an unmarried girl, had carried twins in her arms while other "converts" maintained their distance, was disconcerting to my mother's mother. It meant that no Igbo would marry my mother, which in turn meant an economic loss to my mother's father, who was expecting the bridewealth. It meant that my mother's mother, who was never a "love wife," would be more than ever estranged from her husband, as well as a

---

[3] A residential unit, a homestead, varying in size and population according to the social status of the compound head. A typical Igbo compound is surrounded by a fence or a mud wall which encloses a cluster of huts belonging to different household units and is marked by a large roomy entrance hut (*ovu*) used as a lounge.

target of gossip among her fellow co-wives. Life became unbearable for my mother, who was by now completely rejected by her own mother. My mother made a desperate decision. She is not sure of the year, but from other incidents, I place it at about 1925. She decided to marry in a non-Igbo community. Okrika was her chosen town. In those days to be married at Okrika was synonymous with being sold. Accompanied by my mother's brother, who represented the interests of my mother's mother, and other delegates appointed by my mother's father, my mother travelled on foot to Okrika, an island off the coast, about seventy-five miles from her home. At that time the railway, motor cars, and bicycles were unknown. Considering the circuitous nature of the then existing route, the journey, which lasted four days, must have been more than one hundred miles.

At Okrika, my mother was married to one Jumbo, a wealthy slaveowner, who made her a "love wife." She later gave birth to Igbudiki, my half sister. What appeared to have been a happy married life for my mother was ended with the death of my mother's mother about 1928. She learned of it from friends, but not from Jumbo. In a matter of weeks, she secretly left Okrika, taking my three-year-old half sister with her. By the time Jumbo came for my mother she had decided on divorce. Jumbo then took custody of his daughter, leaving the bride-wealth with the Ayaba Native Court. From all I can gather, the judges who granted the divorce shared the bridewealth among themselves.

This is the background of the opposition of my father's family to his marrying "a woman from Okrika." In their view, a woman who had been spoiled by the luxuries of "salt water" Okrika would find adjustment difficult in "dry land" Igbo. Events proved my father right and his family wrong. "The woman from Okrika who was believed barren has six children," I have heard my mother brag. (My mother has three boys and three girls, excluding the daughter at Okrika.) There is no doubt that my birth in 1930 relieved the anxiety of my parents. My name, Chikezie ("May God Create Well"), is symbolic of what I meant to them. My family's confidence was doubled when the diviner returned his verdict that I was Ufɔmadu reincarnated. Ufɔmadu was my father's immediate older brother, the third of the four sons of my father's mother. On his deathbed, he had advised my father to marry quickly for "he was coming back to him." The diviner's verdict could not be doubted: I have "birthmarks" (three black spots on the right side of my belly) to vindicate it! It is claimed by my father that my "birthmarks" resulted from the marks made on Ufɔmadu *post mortem* for the purpose of vindicating his "personality" in the next cycle of life, which I now represent.

I grew up in a village group called Nsirimo, where there are five lineages (villages). Nsirimo is on the eastern side of the Imo River and had a population of 3999 according to the 1952 census. (We have since contested this figure because of our underrepresentation in a wider political community erroneously termed the Ubakala Clan Council.) In my own world of the lineage, I remember growing up in a big compound dominated by Ogbonna, my father's oldest brother. I did not know my father's mother (who was my mother in my previous life), but I knew her three surviving sons, including my father. Our extended family was a closely knit and very competitive unit. Ogbonna was the most distinguished of his brothers, both in material wealth and in prestige. He claimed "first" in many institutions and title societies. Though he died a poor man (like most Igbo "prestige hunters"), he never lacked prestige. He was very aggressive and often bullied his two younger brothers. Ogbonna never agreed with my mother because of her defiant attitude and uncompromising demand that he share with his brothers while he was still alive the "family property" (which was my father's mother's property). This was a sensitive question about which it was difficult to ascertain my father's views. He was always silent on this matter.

Although I used to enjoy them, I was never involved in the extended family quarrels. Ogbonna loved me. Probably he had no choice: I was not only his brother's son but his brother during my last life cycle on earth. His children were all grown and I was the only boy in the compound qualified by reason of age to be his page. As his page, he took me to all meetings and ceremonials. I carried his medicine bag and listened to his stories. He knew much about our culture and told it to anybody who would listen. He told me what he could remember about our lineage, the wealth of his mother, the feuds in our lineage, and the coming of the white man.

In my lineage growing up was not a traumatic experience. I played with my mates with the toys we improvised. We made traps with which to snare and kill rats. In our spare time we hunted rabbits and we helped with farmwork and entertained ourselves with folk stories and songs in the night. Since my mother had female children late in her life, she forced me to perform the chores normally done by girls. "You are my own daughter," she would insist. It was at this period that she began to explain the circumstances of her first marriage and how my half sister had been left behind at Okrika. I longed to have sisters but none came until 1943.

If village life was placid, schooling in my days was not. There was "learning with tears" rather than "learning with pleasure." Discipline was rigid. Many boys who could have done well were "whipped out of school." I survived schooling through the intervention of my mother. One day she said to our teacher, "Instead of flogging Chikezie, come to my kitchen and flog me." She was serious and the teacher sensed it. Though I was spared the teacher's cane, I had the taunts of my schoolmates to combat. They told everyone that I had a wife. This embarrassed and humiliated me. My mother was then a "big" trader and she needed someone to help in our house and so she "married" one wife after another.[4] When I complained, she assured me that the wife was hers and did not hesitate to tell our teacher so. From my own point of view, this was making the matter worse. I knew from experience how our teachers used to tell boys who failed to get their sums right that they were thinking of their wives at home. Of all my mother's wives (she married them serially) I loved Goodness most. She was my mother's first wife and was ten years my senior. She helped to prepare me for school. Goodness was later married to my father in spite of my mother's opposition. She had difficulty bearing children. After two stillbirths, she divorced

---

[4] "Woman marriage," a recognized institution among the Igbo, enables female "husbands" to acquire rights in other women (who become their "brides") and to play the social roles of a father. For more details, refer to Chapter 5, page 50.

my father for failing to perform the necessary sacrifice to make her childbearing normal. She has five children by her present husband and wept when she last saw me.

By the time I finished grade school, my father had plunged into debt. He was one of the "big six" at the head of a contribution club, into which he had ploughed all the family resources. Then came a big crash—for us a stock market crash. The club "failed" and contributors who had not received their takeout shares sued my father (see chapter 9). My father ran off to Okrika, where he did odd jobs. He sent money to pay off the court fees and to make installment payments to his many contributor-creditors. He learned about my half sister and made sacrifices to the spirit of my mother's former husband which was tormenting her in dreams. Although he was able to pay his debts, my father did not prosecute his own debtors. My mother exploited this weakness in my father whenever they quarreled.

Financially unable to afford a high school education, I became a grade school teacher in 1946. This was not a serious loss; rather, it was a sentimental one. In my village group it was rare for boys of my generation to go to high school. There were only two boys who had been to high school before this time and neither was from my own village. We were expected to be mission teachers after completing grade school. Teaching brought me into contact with a wider Igbo community and opened new experiences. For the first time I was completely alone—without kinsmen and villagers. I was, however, aware of my new status. My monthly salary was fifteen shillings—about $2.25. It would have meant much in purchasing power in those days if the salary could have been regular.

December, 1946, brought me new kinship ties. My mother was then "seeing things"; her former husband, especially, came regularly in her dreams. We decided to visit Okrika, and this we did without my father's blessing. It was my first trip to Port Harcourt, and I enjoyed the long train ride. At Okrika, we stopped at the house of Joseph Opih, who was married to my lineage sister. Mr. Opih became our middleman, a role he played very successfully. In a matter of a few hours news of our arrival reached my half sister at her Iwoma residence. After the Okrika-Ogu riots two years before, my half sister and her husband left Okrika Island for Iwoma, a "dry land" village. It was a dramatic moment for my mother to see her daughter after twenty years of separation. My mother hugged, kissed, and wept over her daughter, but I betrayed no emotion. I had now accomplished my objective: I had given my mother emotional satisfaction; and I had extended not only the bonds of kinship but its obligations. Before we ate dinner, my mother took water and, pouring it out, called on the high God, the spirits of Okrika, and the earth-Goddess of my town, to witness the ritual separation between her and her former husband as well as the new tie forged between her and her daughter. My half sister joined our mother in this ritual and called on her father to keep away from our mother. I noticed that the emotional health of my mother improved after this journey, for she ceased complaining about seeing her former husband in dreams.

I was admitted to a four-year teachers' training college after I had taught in grade schools for five years. Two years earlier, I had married, according to

Igbo custom, a young girl in her third year of the eight-year grade school course. It became my duty, after her bridewealth payment was made, to educate her according to my choice and means. My mother had demanded a grownup girl but I overruled her. Maintaining me at the teachers' training college and my wife and my brother at grade school was not easy for my family but it was done. Following the completion of my training, I was appointed to teach in a high school and I taught in my alma mater for four years. This was a period of great responsibility for me. My town regarded me as one of the emergent elite and treated me accordingly. My family expected me to justify the investment my education represented; my friends and fellow teachers wanted me to qualify for admission to a university. All these were legitimate but conflicting demands following Igbo patterns.

My town demanded leadership from me. But this leadership is a trying as well as a thankless experience. My town has a passionate desire "to get up." There is nothing unique about this; every Igbo community wants to "get up," but no two agree on the methods, to the great detriment of the generally agreed-upon goals. We have made what we culturally define as "progress": three grade schools, five churches, a marketplace, and many village halls. These plants have been built and maintained by our community of four thousand to demonstrate our solidarity to rival groups, both in and outside the village. This is the social setting in which I found myself when I was the secretary of my town's Teachers' and Students' Union and the general secretary of the Nsirimo Improvement Union. The latter has branches in major Nigerian cities and meets twice a year, the more important session being at Christmas. My rural background should be clear to the reader by now. Except for my three years at the University of Ibadan (I spent all my vacations in Igbo country), I have not lived or worked in an urban setting.

When I started ethnographic reading seriously at Ibadan, I realized that I had been an ethnologist without knowing it and I became convinced that I could make my culture more intelligible to others if I acquired the necessary training in social anthropology. As I read more widely, I observed that the culture-bearer's point of view was (and is) absent from this literature. The "native" point of view presented by a sympathetic foreign ethnologist who "knows" his natives is not the same as the view presented by a native. Both views are legitimate, but the native's point of view is yet to enrich our discipline. The argument that a culture-bearer must be assigned only the role of an "educated informant" grows less and less persuasive. Many anthropologists acquire a cross-cultural perspective through reading and participating in foreign cultures, that is, knowing more than one culture at firsthand. The latter should not be confused with "living" more than one culture. Very few people are in a position to do this. Not even the celebrated ethnographer Malinowski could be credited with this: his stay of two years and seven months in the Trobriand Islands was not enough to produce a Trobriander. To "live" a culture demands more than a knowledge of its events' system and institutions; it requires growing up with these events and being emotionally involved with cultural values and biases.

The culture-bearer anthropologist faces some reporting problems. First, from the wealth of data he may be so highly selective that he ignores what appears to him to be commonplace in his culture but is nevertheless relevant to the understanding of that culture. Selectivity, however, is not a unique problem: all ethnographers play an editorial role that involves some degree of data selection. Second, he is emotionally involved in his culture, especially in regard to its "sensitive" zones. This fact has been advanced as a reason why he should be restricted to the role of an educated informant. But his emotional involvement is in itself relevant to our science: it guides the reader in his assessment of the writer, and, methodologically, it can help us to determine the degree of objectivity (when we know how) with which social scientists in general approach sensitive topics in other areas of human behavior. Third, there is the problem of conflict for the culture-bearer anthropologist reporting to a wider audience. He tends to treat with respect and great restraint data that he obtains simply because he "belongs." How much of these data he can use without bursting the core remains a problem. With the advantage of his intimate knowledge, however, he can point out some speculative ethnographies on esoteric aspects of his culture where "what the ethnographer should be told" passes as esoteric lore.

Objectivity is the aim of our science. Every ethnographic writer tries to attain it. Our personalities, the data available to us, and our theoretical position affect our objectivity; hence only the reader can decide how objective I have been in reporting Igbo society and culture.

A few phonetic symbols are necessary in spelling Igbo words. An orthography of these symbols appears in the appendix.

The first chapter—"The Igbo World"—sets the orientation of this study, a study which is structured on the way the Igbo view and "manipulate" their world.

1

The Igbo World

To KNOW HOW a people view the world around them is to understand how they evaluate life; and a people's evaluation of life, both temporal and nontemporal, provides them with a "charter" of action, a guide to behavior. The Igbo world, in all its aspects—material, spiritual, and sociocultural —is made intelligible to Igbo by their cosmology, which explains how everything came into being. Through it, the Igbo know what functions the heavenly and earthly bodies have and how to behave with reference to the gods, the spirits, and the ancestors. In their conception, not only is cosmology an explanatory device and a guide to conduct; it is also an action system. As an explanatory device, Igbo cosmology theorizes about the origin and character of the universe. I am not concerned with this aspect of the Igbo world view here. Rather, I am concerned with two other aspects: cosmology as a system of prescriptive *ethics,* which defines what the Igbo ought to do and what they ought to avoid; and cosmology as an *action system,* which reveals what the Igbo actually do as manifested in their overt and covert behavior. The latter is very important if we are to understand the dynamic factors in Igbo culture. But the three aspects of Igbo cosmology must not be regarded as isolated phenomena. They are interrelated. I have isolated them for analytical purposes, as a way of organizing the data and illustrating this well-accepted fact: that cosmological ideas express the basic notions underlying cultural activities and define cultural goals and social relations.

The World of Man and the World of Spirits

The Igbo world is a "real" one in every respect. There is the world of man peopled by all created beings and things, both animate and inaminate. The spirit world is the abode of the creator, the deities, the disembodied and malignant spirits, and the ancestral spirits. It is the future abode of the living after their death. There is constant interaction between the world of man and the

11

world of the dead; the visible and invisible forces. Existence for the Igbo, there-fore, is a dual but interrelated phenomenon involving the interaction between the material and the spiritual, the visible and the invisible, the good and the bad, the living and the dead. The latter are a part of the Igbo social world.

In the Igbo conception, the world of the "dead" is a world full of activities; its inhabitants manifest in their behavior and thought processes that they are "liv-ing." The dead continue their lineage system; they are organized in lineages with patrilineal emphasis just as are those on earth. The principle of seniority makes the ancestors the head of the lineage; it gives the lineage its stability and continu-ity. An Igbo without ɘmɘnna—a patrilineage—is an Igbo without citizenship both in the world of man and in the world of the ancestors. In the Igbo view, there is a constant interaction between the dead and the living: the dead are rein-carnated, death making the transition from the corporeal to the incorporeal life of the ancestors possible. An illustration of the reality of the Igbo dual but inter-related world is provided by this dialogue. Father Shanahan, a great Roman Cath-olic missionary among the Igbo (who later became a bishop), wanted to baptize a condemned murderer before his death.

> MURDERER: "If I accept baptism, Father, will it prevent me from meeting my enemy in the next life?"
> FATHER: "Well, no, you will probably meet him one way or the other."
> MURDERER: "Then baptize me by all means, and as soon as I do meet him, I'll knock his head off a second time" (Jordan, 1949:137).

Apparent in this dialogue is the Igbo conviction that there is a carry-over of social status and other personal qualities from the world of man to the world of the dead. The murderer accepted baptism, not because he believed that it would cleanse his sins but rather because of the reassurance that the baptism was not meant to prevent a face-to-face meeting with his enemy, whose head he want-ed to "knock off a second time," thus demonstrating his physical superiority over his enemy in the world of man and the world of the dead.

For the Igbo, death is a necessary precondition for joining the ancestors, just as reincarnation is necessary for the peopling of the temporal segment of the lineage. Therefore death which occurs at a ripe age is a cause for joy, being an index of high status among the ancestors. But since the young as well as the old die, death is received with mixed feelings. Death is personified and dealt with as a powerful spirit which gains mastery over Ndɘ, the life-giving principle. It is the severance of this life-giving principle from the human, corporeal body. Without death, there will be no population increase in the ancestral households and correspondingly, no change in social status for the living Igbo.

Maintaining Cosmological Balance

The world as a natural order which inexorably goes on its ordained way according to a "master plan" is foreign to Igbo conceptions. Rather, their world is a dynamic one—a world of moving equilibrium. It is an equilibrium that is constantly threatened, and sometimes actually disturbed by natural and social calamities. The events which upset it include natural disasters like long, continuous droughts, long periods of famine, epidemic diseases, as well as sorcery and other antisocial forces; litigation, homicide, violation of taboo, and other incidents which the Igbo define as *Nsɔ* or *Alɵ*—taboo.

But the Igbo believe that these social calamities and cosmic forces which disturb their world are controllable and should be "manipulated" by them for their own purpose. The maintenance of social and cosmological balance in the world becomes, therefore, a dominant and pervasive theme in Igbo life. They achieve this balance, for instance, through divination, sacrifice, appeal to the countervailing powers of their ancestors (who are their invisible father-figures) against the powers of the malignant, and nonancestral spirits, and, socially, through constant realignment in their social groupings.

Death, for example, disturbs the existing social and ritual relationships and demands a new mode of adjustment for the bereaved family. The status goal of the one who dies young seems frustrated, and in his family creates a vacuum in its role structure through the loss of a member. The uncertainty about the cause of such an untimely death is a source of concern for all. Divination settles this uncertainty by specifying the cause of death and recommending ritual remedies. The diviner's verdicts follow a culturally expected pattern: the deaths of young people are usually blamed on the sins committed during their previous life on earth; deaths of adults may be attributed to "ripe" age, or senility, a breach of taboo or other antisocial behavior, such as sorcery, false oath, or theft committed in his previous or present life. Whatever the verdict, the loss of ritual balance is implicit and ritual remedies are recommended. If sorcery is involved, the deceased adult is denied "ground" burial (a privilege accorded only to those who die without blemish), and the corpse is cast into *ɔhia ɔjɔɔ*—a "bad bush" fit only for the outcast. The ritual purifications are primarily designed to dissociate the living from the deceased's blemish and thus reestablish the ritual balance his breach of taboo has destroyed.

Indeed, whatever threatens the life of the individual or his security as well as society is interpreted by the Igbo as a sign of warning that things must be set right before they get out of hand. Losses in trade indicate to the trader that his *Mbataku*—the wealth-bringing deity—is threatening action for being neglected, while drought or too long a rainy season is a warning that society has lost its balance with nature.

Not only deities and spiritual forces are manipulated. Human beings and social relations are also subject to manipulation. As we shall see in Chapter 7, the Igbo individual balances his conflicts in one agnatic group with his privileges in another. His *umunɛ* (mother's agnates[1] among whom he enjoys *okɛnɛ* privileges) stand with him against the perennial conflicts he

---

[1] Agnates are patrilateral kinsfolk. They are men and women to whom one is related through males only. In other words, a descent link from a man to a child is called an *agnatic* link while a descent link from a woman to a child is called *uterine* link. A social group tracing descent through males only is an *agnatic group*.

faces among his *ɵmɵnna* (his own agnates). Although he is exposed to physical danger among his *ɵmɵnna,* his person is sacred in his *umunɛ.* It is the place of his exile should he be convicted of sorcery by his *ɵmɵnna.* Assured of the support of a strong *umunɛ,* the Igbo can challenge his *ɵmɵnna* successfully; with the support of both his *ɵmɵnna* and his *umunɛ,* he can move his world.

When we come to the domain of Igbo legal process, the same principle of balance of forces is seen at work. Legal procedures aim essentially at readjusting social relations. Social justice is more than law, and the spirit of the law is more important than the letter of the law: this seems to be the Igbo juridicial principle. The resolution of a case does not have to include a definite victory for one of the parties involved. Judgment among the Igbo ideally involves a compromise. They insist that a good judgment "cuts into the flesh as well as the bone" of the matter under dispute. This implies a "hostile" compromise in which there is neither victor nor vanquished; a reconciliation to the benefit of—or a loss to—both parties.

Those relationships not considered mutually beneficial tend to remain fragile. Parties to a relationship, whether they are human or spiritual, are expected to fulfill some obligation and to derive some reward. Each party is expected to be motivated by self-interest. The relationship lasts as long as the parties are satisfied with the terms of the contract. As the Igbo proverb puts it, "It is only proper that the left and right palms should wash each other so that both might be clean."

Underlying the maxim that social life demands "beneficial reciprocity" is the realization that no individual or spirit is self-sufficient. Human interdependence is a constant theme in the folklore of the Igbo. It is the greatest of all values for them. As another proverb has it: "A man is never so stout that flesh covers his nails." "To help one to get up" is an ever-recurring theme in their social life. A man who "helps others to get up" commands much prestige. He is the "big" man, the popular man who deserves much respect and obedience. Since the need to get along well with everyone is such a major concern in interpersonal relations, a properly socialized Igbo is one who is able to interact with others, to speak out his mind freely even if it hurts to do so. Getting on well with neighbors does not mean "letting them alone." What one person does is of great concern to others. It is the Igbo way to associate with people who will give one advice, to have friends "who can hear one's cry." Secretive persons who "bury injuries in their minds" are held in contempt; they are often the victims of unwarranted aggression and targets of sorcery accusations. They hinder social adjustment through human interdependence.

The world of man and the world of spirits are also interdependent. Between them there is always some form of interdependence, a beneficial reciprocity. The principle of reciprocity demands that the ancestors be honored and offered regular sacrifice, and be "fed" with some crumbs each time the living take their meal; it also imposes on the ancestors the obligation of "prospering" the lineage, protecting its members, and standing with them as a unit against the machinations of wicked men and malignant spirits. The same principle requires that all spirits and deities whose help is invoked during a period of crisis and who stand firm throughout it be rewarded with appropriate sacrifice.

Because reciprocity is the organizing principle of Igbo social relationship, near equality is their ideal. Domination by a few powerful men or spirits is deeply resented. A relationship that is one-sided, either in its obligation or in its reward system, does not last long among them. Imbalance, either in the social or in the spiritual world, is considered a trouble indicator. Through mutual interdependence and his ability to manipulate his world, the Igbo individual tries to achieve equality or near equality in both the world of man and the world of the spirits.

Manipulating His World

The Igbo world is not only a world in which people strive for equality; it is one in which change is constantly expected. Its contractual character makes it a constantly changing world. Since the relationship between the social world and the spiritual world is contractual, there is always the fear that the terms of the contract might not be fully honored by either party: the spirits often change their mind as do men. Each tries to get the better part of the other, a source of uncertainty in Igbo social relations. This uncertainty is not critical for the Igbo. It simply keeps him alert since he believes that social relations can be manipulated. For every force, he tries to provide a countervailing force. He achieves this either through shifting his alliance or by invoking the aid of a more powerful force.

If you ask the Igbo why he believes that the world should be manipulated, he will reply "The world is a marketplace and it is subject to bargain." In his view, neither the world of man alone nor the world of the spirits is a permanent home. The two worlds together constitute a home. Each world is peopled with "interested" individuals and groups and much buying and selling goes on in each. People go to the marketplace for different reasons, but the common motivation is the desire to make a profit. Although the profit motive is the guiding factor, there are occasional losses. From the Igbo point of view, a person does not abandon trading because he suffers losses. It would be cowardly to do so, but he cannot carry on indefinitely if he does not balance his losses with gains. The Igbo would advise the perennially unsuccessful trader to change his line of merchandise. Instead of trading in yams, he should try pepper; eventually he will find his line. But if all else fails, magic will not.

This description of life in the idiom of market exchange is not a mere theoretical formulation of mine; it is the Igbo way and is manifested in their everyday behavior. This idiom is dramatized every time a mother goes to the village market. She has packed her wares in a rectangular wicker basket. As she is helped to put the load on her head, her children, who are hanging around to give her the "market wish," come up one after the other and say:

Nnε zugbuo ndi ahia;
Ndi ahia azugbula gi.

This may be rendered as:

> Mother, gain from market people;
> Market people, lose to mother.

As each child gives his market wish, he spits into the mother's cupped palms. When this ritual is over, mother rubs her palms together and ritually cleanses her face, thus symbolically, ensuring "good face" for the day's bargaining operations. An interesting feature of the market wish ritual is that it conforms to the principle of social balance. Among the Igbo, market prices are determined by a rigorous system of bargaining, a time-consuming operation from the Westerner's point of view. It is a bargain between a buyer and a seller, each of whom is consciously dramatizing the market wish.

Cyclical Nature of Status Seeking

It is a fair assessment of the Igbo world to say that the most important commodity it offers and for which the Igbo strive is the ɔzɔ, or title system. The Igbo are status seekers. To use a market metaphor, they believe that the world is a marketplace where status symbols can be bought.

For the Igbo, life on earth is a link in the chain of status hierarchy which culminates in the achievement of ancestral honor in the world of the dead. In this view, those who die young suffer much frustration in Ala Mmθɔ —the spirit land. They remain "boys" in both worlds—most repugnant to Igbo youth. Fortunately for the low-status person, this is temporary because the Igbo believe in reincarnation. A person's social position is such an important thing that even on his deathbed the individual Igbo thinks more of his status in the hereafter than of his death. His most important injunctions to his heir and family are: Do not shame my spirit. Do not let my enemies see my corpse. Give me good burial. For the Igbo, status-seeking is a cyclical process of death, individual role bargaining with the creator, reincarnation, birth, and then death.

The social importance of reincarnation is that it provides the "idea system" that rationalizes, interprets, accommodates, or rejects changes and innovations as well as tolerates certain character traits. Furthermore, it is at reincarnation that the individual works out a proper role for himself through face-to-face interaction with the creator. Guided by his *chi*—the Igbo form of guardian spirit—the reincarnating soul makes a choice from two parcels that *chinɛkɛ*, the creator, presents. Of these two parcels, one is believed to contain the desired social positions that the individual predicted in his *ɛbibi* (preincarnation social position that the individual predicts during his lifetime on earth). In their *ɛbibi*, most Igbo predict long life, intelligence, wealth, "having mouth," that is, the power of oratory and wisdom. What the Igbo seldom realize is that these desirable traits are not genetically or spiritually transmitted but are the result of conditioning through their child-rearing practices, which are constantly reinforced by rewards and sanctions of adults as well as by the general demands made on the individual Igbo by his culture.

Not all Igbo are able to make the "right" choice in their role bargaining with the creator. A "wrong" choice, however, does not spell the social doom of the reincarnating Igbo. He can still make the most of his choice while on earth and hope for better luck during the next cycle.

Transparent Living

In a world where life processes are delicately balanced, and where the individual has a wide latitude in manipulating human and nonhuman elements to his possible advantage, it is necessary for people to live *transparent lives*. We have mentioned earlier that secretive persons are held in contempt as not being properly socialized; that the Igbo group-oriented value system does not imply a "let alone" policy in interpersonal relations. There are conflicts. To resolve them, adjustment through compromise is the accepted way. To achieve this compromise the cause of the conflict must be made known to arbitrators. Anybody can play this role.

Igbo are a people who tend to wash their dirty linen in public. Anyone who has overheard Igbo co-wives quarreling will appreciate this point. The compact household units, the matter-of-fact approach to sex, the symbolic way "transparency" is conveyed by tasting food or drink meant for the visitor or neighbor, the respect accorded to the leader who has "strong eyes" to see "hidden things" and the "mouth" to expose them are indicative of their "transparent" orientation. The concept of the good life among the Igbo is so built on the transparency theme that the individual dreads any form of loss of face. The major deterrent to crime is not guilt-feeling but shame-feeling.

The qualities demanded of Igbo leaders emphasize their transparent orientation. The leader should be accessible to all. If he holds *ɔfɔ*—the symbol of ritual authority—he is required to vindicate his innocence regularly through the rite of *iju ogu*—the affirmation of innocence. This is generally regarded as a formal indication that he maintains his ritual status—a necessary condition for his high office. To dispel suspicion and reassure themselves that no evil is planned, two friends whose relations are strained may resort to *igbandu*—a formal oath for re-establishing confidence—in which one may drink the blood of the other. A stranger may be required to swear repeatedly to his host, a husband will swear with his wife's lover (concubinage is one of the institutions for sexual expression among Igbo), and patron-client relationships as well as doctor-patient relationships may be strengthened by repeated swearing of fidelity. In this context, the experience of a female British anthropologist who worked in an Igbo village-group is worth citing: "The elders of the village, in spite of the fact that some of them were nervous lest a white woman might have designs upon their land and palm trees, were nonetheless convinced that if she decided to decamp they would be ridiculed by the surrounding villages. They were therefore always urging me to swear with them that I would not go away" (Green 1947:252). This demonstrable evidence of good faith is the pattern of behavior one would expect from a people who put so much value on transparent living and who are realistic enough to believe that some people will not live up to the ideal behavior unless they are constrained to do so.

Furthermore, the period of nudity, which once extended into adolescence for both boys and girls, was a symbolic expression of their "transparent" character, since girls were expected to be virgins at marriage. Most personal acts like *iyi ɔgwo*—the acquisition of protective medicine, and the borrowing or lending of money—are usually done in the presence of witnesses. To hide these facts would lead to the suspicion that dangerous medicine was being acquired and that money was being borrowed for antisocial purposes. As I have mentioned in a different context earlier, solitude is regarded as a mark of wickedness, of evil design. Of course, not every Igbo lives up to this ideal. To be a properly socialized Igbo is to approximate "as far as the eye can see"—the Igbo way.

"A Country Is Spoiled By Men"

A proverb often cited by Igbo elders and judges is *Madu bɵ njɔ ala*—"Man makes the country wicked." It is man who "spoils" the country and not the spirits, the people emphasize.

An Igbo anecdote gives the basis of this maxim and its implication for their transparent orientation. It is told of an Igbo leader and philosopher who was engaged in an informal discussion with a distinguished foreign visitor who made some disparaging remark about his host's country. This comment upset the philosopher, who thought about it for a while and then made this reply:

"Do you say that my country is bad? Can the earth or trees or mud walls speak? How do they offend?"

"No," the visitor answered. "As far as I know, they don't."

"Well answered," the philosopher replied. "Never speak badly of my country again. Should any of my people offend you, accuse them directly."

As if to leave no doubt in the mind of the visitor, the philosopher called one of his sons, by name Madubunjɔala, and requested him to bring *ɔkwa*—a carved wooden bowl for presenting pepper and kola nut. After his son had left, the philosopher explained: "To mark the intrigues of some of my enemies in this country, I named that child (pointing after his son) *Madubunjɔala* ('Man makes a country wicked'). It is people and not spirits who make a country 'wicked.'"

This anecdote clearly indicates the direction of scapegoating among the Igbo. When things go wrong, people of "shady" character—solitary and secretive persons—are accused. This logically follows from the transparency theme. The reasoning may be briefly stated: The ideal of a transparent life is incompatible with antisocial behavior. Those who live a "dark" life are the enemies of society because they commit most crimes.

A World of Change

The Igbo world is one in which change is expected. Change is accepted as a realistic adjustment to the status and role structure, as an adjustment to the world around them. I mentioned earlier the Igbo belief in reincarnation and its implication for the individual role bargaining with the creator. It appears to me that the latter is the most important ideological factor making for internally induced change among the Igbo. Believing that he chose his roles, the Igbo is constrained to make a success of his social position or career. This belief, too, imposes on his family the obligation of providing the sociocultural environment for the realization of his status goals. In effect, the Igbo stress on the success goal is ideologically rooted in the reincarnation dogma.

Though the quest for success goals is full of hazards and sometimes a threat to life, this fact does not deter the Igbo. "One who is overcautious of his life is always killed by the fall of a dry leaf," they say. It is their view that life must be faced and its problems overcome. Facing life's challenges may involve physical aggression, the use of protective medicine, or even bribery. To protect one's rights in a changing world requires perpetual vigilance. "An absentee child," they say, "eats his yam half roasted." In a world of equals like the Igbo, where all the people are competing for the same goal, the rule of the game is that competitors must be alert if they hope to win.

The individual freedom of choice fostered by Igbo culture allows innovation. There is opportunity for experimentation as well as tolerance for failure and admiration for success. The most important factor for the acceptance or rejection of an innovation is its status implication for the individuals and groups concerned. The crucial question is this: Will the acceptance of this innovation "make the individual or the town get up"? If the answer is in the affirmative, there is a great possibility of immediate acceptance; but to be retained, the innovation "must work," the material and symbolic evidence of "getting up" must be demonstrated.

Equalitarianism

The Igbo world in based on an equalitarian principle. Equality or near equality ensures that no one person or group of persons acquires too much control over the life of others. This is an ideological obstacle to the development of a strong central authority. However, no human society achieves absolute equality among its citizens and Igbo society is no exception. There are distinctions of age, sex, and wealth. The Igbo realize this quite well and, in fact, stress these factors in their stratification model. What the Igbo mean by an equalitarian society is that which gives to all its citizens an equal opportunity to achieve success. The stress is on achievement. They recognize that "a child who washes his hands clean deserves to eat with his elders."

The Igbo achievement orientation has two important social effects. In the first place, it makes the Igbo world a highly competitive one in which the rules of competition may be manipulated by the status seeker in order to attain his goals. Second, it fosters a sociopolitical system which is conciliar and democratic. A forward-moving and talented young man who can acquire wealth and "convert" it into the traditionally valued status symbols (such as title taking) is allowed to wield political power over his peers and elders. This is a further demonstration of the Igbo saying that "no one knows the womb that bears the chief." It is not surprising that chiefship among the Igbo must not only be achieved, but be constantly validated to be retained.

The Igbo leader "emerges": he is not born or made. The Igbo saying that "everyone is a chief in his hut" must be understood in its proper context. What is meant is that a dictatorial leader of the Igbo is inconceivable. A leader may be a dictator if he likes, but his leadership must be restricted to his household. A leader is supported by his followers as long as "he does not govern too much." To govern too much is to alienate them. As long as a leader behaves as if he is making it possible for everyone "to get up," that is, to advance their social status, so long will he remain an ideal leader. Within this context, indeed, a leader may have his way as well as enjoy the support of followers. This is the typical situation which makes the Igbo hero worshipers.

Igbo leadership depends on the concept of public service and the realization of dreams: high status for the individual and progress for the community. The town is a small village-group in which the leader operates. His ability to influence any other similar unit is minimal. Each village-group is suspicious of, and often hostile to, the neighboring village-groups. "A tall tree does not span two towns" is an Igbo proverb that makes sense in a highly segmented society. Since political office is not remunerative, an aggressive expansionist policy does not have much meaning for the Igbo. Their expansion has been small and predatory. Dwelling units are villages rather than semiurban units; sociopolitical integration is achieved through decentralization rather than through hierarchical organization.

Summary

The Igbo world is a world peopled by the invisible and visible forces, by the living, the dead, and those yet to be born. It is a world in which all these forces interact, affecting and modifying behavior; a world that is delicately balanced between opposing forces, each motivated by its self-interest; a world whose survival demands some form of cooperation among its members, although that cooperation may be minimal and even hostile in character. It is a world in which others can be manipulated for the sake of the individual's status advancement— the goal of Igbo life. It conceives reincarnation as not only the bridge between the living and the dead, but a necessary precondition for the transaction and transfer of social status from the world of man to the world of the dead. It is a world of constant struggle which recognizes that conflict situations exist and therefore demands from the individual constant adjustments; and, although leaving some of the rules of adjustment rather vague, still insists that "good citizenship" demands "transparent" living and that human interdependence is the greatest of all values. It is a world that is spoiled by man and not by spirits; yet man is allowed a wide latitude in his behavior—an important factor in the dynamics of Igbo culture. Finally, it is a world in which the leader is given minimal power and yet is expected to give maximum service in return—the hallmark of which is "to make the town get up." This is the Igbo world.

2

How the Igbo Make Their Living

THE IGBO have a "root crop" economy. Yam, cassava (manioc), and many varieties of cocoyam (taro) are the chief staples and provide the bulk of the population with most subsistence needs. No meal is considered to be complete without at least one or two of them. These staples have a high yield which is offset to some extent by their long growth period. Only one crop is possible in a year's farming cycle. Their profitable cultivation requires abundant land and cheap labor. Land being the chief factor in food production, a description of how these staples are grown must start with the Igbo system of land tenure.

Land means many things to the Igbo. It is the domain of the earth-goddess, a burial place for the ancestors, a place to live on and make a living. Land is therefore the most important asset to the people. It is a source of security which is emotionally protected from alienation. It is believed that a people cannot have too much land and that no opportunity to acquire rights in land should be lost.

Farming: Land Tenure

The system of land tenure used by the Igbo prescribes the rights of individuals or groups over the land they use, how such rights may be acquired, their content, the security enjoyed in them, what transfers can be made, and the succession to them. The Igbo system of land tenure is based on four principles: (1) All land is owned. There is no concept of "abandonment of land" or "no man's land" among the Igbo. Whether land is cultivated or not, it belongs to somebody. (2) Land ultimately belongs to the lineage and cannot be alienated from it. As we shall see later, this is a statement of ideology rather than of fact. Actually, the Igbo have institutionalized ways of alienating land. (3) Within his lineage, the individual has security of tenure for the land he needs for building his house and making his farms. (4) No member of the lineage is without land. The implementation of the last principle has led to fragmentation of land.

Briefly, six systems of land tenure may be distinguished. (1) The chief basis of transmission of land rights is through inheritance. Generally this is from father to son. Because they must marry away, women do not normally inherit land in this way but they acquire rights in land in other ways. (2) There is what is called "kola tenancy," by which rights in land are transferred for little or no consideration other than the gift of kola from the tenant to the grantor. The gift of kola is not a purchase price, and the grantor reserves the right of reversion on the death of the kola tenant or the absence of heirs. With scarcity of land causing much litigation over the right of reversion, kola tenancy now takes the form of a "showing" tenure, in which a grantor "shows" a piece of land to a tenant for one farming season and a different piece of land in another season if it is needed, thus indicating unequivocally that only usufructuary rights are involved.[1] (3) A lease-hold gives usufructuary rights to tenants for one or more farming seasons, usually at a consideration reflecting the economic value of land at that place. Anybody can acquire a leasehold. Unlike kola tenancy, "showing" tenure, or a pledge, a leasehold is not terminable at the whim of the grantor. (4) A pledge is the most common type of land tenure. It is a transaction in which a lender of money obtains a temporary usufructuary interest in a piece of land as security for his loan. The land remains perpetually redeemable by the borrower or pledgor on repayment of the loan. This is a flexible contract. Land acquired on pledge may be repledged to a third party provided the initial capital is not exceeded. The pledgee may not plant permanent trees or build on the land. Economic trees like oil palm and iroko may or may not be part of the pledge. There is no compensation for improvement effected by the pledgee in the land. It can be redeemed at any time but the pledgee is entitled to harvest crops growing on the land. (5) Contrary to what the Igbo say, the permanent transfer of rights or interests in land in consideration of some livestock or a sum of money (in modern times) is neither unknown nor a recent development. Its incidence is small and where it occurs, it is usually denied. There is evidence that land was sold to pay fines in title societies, as compensation for homicide, and, in recent times, to kinsmen who wanted to build "country" homes. In each of those cases the landlord gives the buyer a handful of sand in exchange for a goat which is killed on the land to appease the ancestors. (6) In some Igbo communities there are plots of land known as ɔfɔ land[2] which are attached to the office of the ɔfɔ holder; its inheritance follows the principle of positional succession to that office. What may be called "communal land" is restricted to Nkpa or ɔhia ɔjɔɔ—the bad bush, in which the "wicked" who were denied "ground burial" were disposed of.

The Igbo system of land tenure is flexible enough to allow strangers, married women, the free born and slaves, to acquire land for farming.

---

[1] A *usufructuary right* over land is a *use right*—the right to cultivate and make use of the products of a given piece of land without a legal claim to the ownership of that land.

[2] ɔfɔ is a staff of ritual authority and comes from a branch of a tree called *Detarium elastica*. A portion of the lineage land which is attached to the ritual office of a lineage or sublineage head is known as ɔfɔ land.

The Farming Cycle

The farming cycle begins between January and February each year at a time when the harmattan wind has "opened up" the bush. The general pattern is a block system in which the villagers make their gardens in one section of the village land each year. The duration of the "bush fallow" reflects the pressure of population on land. In areas of dense population, such as Onitsha, Awka, Orlu, Okigwi, and Mbaise districts, the "bush fallow" period varies from one to three years, whereas a four-year period or more is characteristic of Ikwerre, Ngwa, and Umuahia. Men clear the bush with machetes. Tree tops are lopped by expert climbers. Sticks for staking yams are collected during bush clearing. Green leaves are allowed to lie on the ground to dry, where they are later burned to form an ash base, the chief source of fertilizer.

Planting starts with the first rains, which generally occur in late March or early April. When the rains seem to fail, the village rain maker (who makes rain in the dry season and drives it away in the rainy season) is paid by the villagers to make rain. Planting is a collective activity in which division of labor by age and sex and skill is marked. Among the southern Igbo planting is done with two implements—the *ubε* and the *ɔgɵ*. The *ubε*, a hoe mounted on a long, pliable handle weighted at the top, is used by the men to make cylindrical holes at six-foot intervals. Women and children use the *ɔgɵ*, a small hoe, to scrape the surrounding topsoil containing the "ash base" into each hole. In this a yam seedling is planted by working the topsoil around the filled-in hole until a small yam hill is created. The northern Igbo make larger yam hills which represent a different concession to their soil. These are made by able-bodied men who are skilled at the job.

The economic interest of Igbo women in the farm is so well recognized that the "women's crops follow the men's." Following the planting of yam,[3] the prime crop, plots are allocated to the women individually. Each woman plants such crops as maize, melon, and okra on the slopes of yam hills; and pumpkins, beans, and, sometimes, cassava and cocoyams between the spaces provided by the yam hills. This system, known as *intercropping,* where three or more crops, maturing at different times are grown on the same plot of land, is well suited to a "hoe culture" where exposure of the soil invites its erosion. While the women are busy planting their crops, men stake the growing yams. From this period on, women's tasks in the garden increase while those of the men are reduced to peri-

---

[3] The West African yam must not be confused with the sweet potato that Americans call "yam." A monocotyledonous twining herb with heavily veined leaves, the West African yam (genus *Dioscorea*) is generally larger than the sweet potato. The Igbo distinguish more than fifteen varieties of yam which are ranked according to their prestige and function in "yam title" rites. A title society is an exclusive club which one joins by paying an entrance fee and feasting the members, thus qualifying for life membership in it. As the result of this, the title taker acquires a "praise name" and is entitled to share the entrance fees of others when they join. "Yam title," one of the many Igbo title institutions, is open to men who have achieved recognition in the production of certain types of yam, the quantity and quality of which are regulated by the yam title society.

odic visits to support the yam vines. Weeding is done twice on each farm and is usually performed by women. The first weeding occurs in April and the second in July or August. In April or May women plant their "special" gardens of either cassava or cocoyams. This is a recent development caused by the fact that even on poor soils cassava has a higher yield than yam, by the demand of the growing city population's for *gari* (cassava flour), and by its relatively low cost of production. The importance of *gari* as the city staple cannot be overestimated. It is easy to prepare and ideally suits the bachelor and migrant. The Igbo who have not lived outside their village still regard it as "Lagos food"—the traveler's food. The association which the Igbo make between *gari* and Lagos is interesting because the *Brazilias,* as the freed slaves who migrated from Brazil to Lagos in 1780 are called, brought the art of preparing *gari* from cassava flour. However, older people still regard *gari* as an inferior food lacking the prestige of yam, the traditional staple. Among the city dwellers who are losing the older dietary preferences and acquiring new ones, *gari* is superseding all other staples in importance but not in prestige.

By June, all the yams have been planted. A period of food shortage called ɵnwɵ sets in. As yams become scarce, men depend on their wives for subsistence. The chief staples then become cassava, cocoyams, and, in some parts of southern Igbo, the three-leaved yam locally known as *cnɵ.* Breadfruit is also important, especially in the Mbaise, Obowo, Okigwi, and Orlu areas. Ɵnwɵ is caused by lack of a well-developed system of storing surplus yams until the new crop is harvested. Men of prestige and high social status keep enough yams for themselves and their visitors, since the prestige of yam is such that Igbo regard cassava meal as the "poor man's food." In many southern Igbo communities the situation is saved by an early variety of yams called *Apu ji* and *ji oko,* which may be harvested twice, beginning in July and August.

Before the final harvests begin, in October, the yam houses, called *ɔba,* have been repaired. The yams are harvested by men and washed and carried home by women and children. Some communities still maintain two separate yam houses: one at the farm and another at home. Yams are first dried in the sun and then tied by specialists to long upright sticks secured to the permanent live posts by means of raphia cord (*akwara*). From the harvest to the end of the next planting season, yam is eaten as often as Americans eat bread. In addition to farm crops, the Igbo add to their diets bananas, breadfruit, plantain, kola nuts, oranges, pears (*ubɛ*), pawpaw, and raphia liquor.[4] The trees providing these supplementary foods are often in separate groves and are individually owned. An important source of food supply, from the nutritional point of view, is obtained by the collection of wild vegetable products of the forest and bush, such as mushroom, ɵkazi, ɵtabazi, and ɵziza. In the densely populated areas where close settlement has reduced the natural vegetation, these wild vegetables are sold in the markets.

Production for exchange is an important feature of Igbo economy. The people have always produced some surplus but only a "restricted sphere" of this

---

[4] Raphia liquor is derived from the sap of the oil palm tree (*Elaeis guineensis*).

production formerly entered the market. Yam production, for instance, is more for prestige than for trade. The goal is to have a full yam house and then to take a yam title. Seed yams are bought and sold, but the traffic in yams (both for domestic consumption and for planting) is small in relation to total production. Of the products which enter the local exchange, palm produce is the chief one; other products from the farm, forest, and local crafts are secondary.

The Preparation of Palm Oil

The production of palm oil and palm kernels is in the hands of the domestic group. Interest in oil palm can be acquired by anybody through sale, lease, or pledge. By means of a single or a double-climbing rope, depending on the locality, the men gather the fruit from oil palms that grow wild or in plantations. The children remove the nuts from the husks, and the women direct the extraction of the oil. Two methods are used: the soft oil and the hard oil processes. In the soft oil process the nuts are boiled in water until they become tender. Then they are pounded by the men in a big mortar (*ikwε*), after which the women and children separate the nuts from the fibers in a rectangular dugout called an *ogbɔ*. The fibers are then pressed over heated pieces of stone to stimulate the flow of oil. The resulting oil, now ready for sale, is stored in gourd containers or empty kerosene tins. In the hard oil process the unboiled nuts are pounded. After water is poured over the pulp the resulting surface oil is skimmed and then boiled. Finally, the oil is drawn off. It is estimated that by the hard oil process about 55 to 60 percent of the oil content is recovered, whereas about 50 percent is recovered by the soft oil process. Nevertheless, the latter method is favored because it yields a better cooking oil, keeps longer, and, as the result of containing less free fatty acid, commands a better price.

The use of hand presses is encouraged by the Regional government. They have become increasingly accepted since World War II. Cheap hand presses giving a 65 percent extraction are in common use but have been generally opposed by Ngwa women, who see in this innovation a threat to their traditional rights in kernels. The Pioneer Oil Mills are even more efficient, giving about 85 percent extraction and a quality of oil with the lowest free fatty acid. For palm fruits the mills depend on plantations and open-market competition.

The women's reward for their cooperation with the men in processing the oil palm fruit is their traditional right to the kernels; the men claim the oil if the fruits belong to them. To extract the kernels, the women and their dependents crush the nuts between stones. This is usually the main work during the rainy season, when there is a short lull in farm tasks and trading is generally not very promising. At each market day, however, the need for cash is a strong incentive to extract the kernels. Women bring to market their farm products, products of their own crafts, such as pots, as well as men's products, such as wooden mortars, wooden ladles, hoes, knives, iron traps, and cordage. European goods and smoked fish from the riverine areas are traded.

Trading

Trading has become an important source of livelihood for the Igbo. It is no longer possible for them to maintain their present standard of living by depending entirely on their agriculture. There are some Igbo communities where trading has superseded farming in importance, but the prestige attached to the farmer who grows his own food is still high. To remind an Igbo that he is *ori mgbɛ ahia lɔrɔ,* "one who eats only what the market holds," is to humiliate him. This does not imply that traders are not respected; all it means is that the Igbo see farming as their chief occupation and trading as subsidiary and not a substitute for it.

Trading has a long history among the Igbo. Trade before European contact was of two types: the rural village market, which was dominated by women and in which exchange was limited to domestic needs; and the long-distance trade within or outside Igbo country, which was dominated by men. The latter trade was important for salt, slaves, horses, the tsetse-resistant *Ndama* and *Muturu* cows, grinding stones, and machine-made goods. Salt came from the delta area, especially from Uburu, an inland village-group. Uburu was also an important marketplace for horses and cows, which came from the north and from the French-speaking West Africa. The marketplaces that were important for slaves, grinding stones, and farm implements included Uzuakoli, Uburu, Amaraku, and Bende.

Under the Colonial Administration as a result of the improvement of roads, the advent of the railways, and the growth of cities, some of the important Igbo markets have lost their traditional status; all have changed in character, some structural changes in market organization have taken place, and the role of the trader has become a specialized one. What were traditionally long-distance markets are local markets today. Some journeys which took weeks now take hours. The commodities in which the long-distance trader commanded a monopoly are sold by many petty traders today. With the abolition of the slave trade such slave markets as Uburu, Uzuakoli, Oguta, and Bende have fallen in importance. New marketplaces have appeared as the result of their central location or access to railway and roads. Umuahia is an example of a new marketplace that has overshadowed the older ones—Uzuakoli and Bende are only twelve miles distant. A discussion of the marketplace is necessary to an understanding of the integrating role of the market institution in Igbo life.

The marketplace is a specific site where buyers and sellers (as well as observers) meet, principally for the purpose of commercial transactions. For the village-group which "owns" the marketplace, it is a great status symbol; for the trader, it is a place for business. Nevertheless, all will agree that it is an important social center with economic and noneconomic functions. It is an important news and gossip center and a place for ceremonials and parades, especially following important second-burial rites, successful swearing of oaths of innocence, and title taking. It is a place to meet a girl to marry, to negotiate a divorce, to make love, to collect one's debt, pay or collect one's contribution, and have a drink with one's age mates, friends, and in-laws.

The Marketplace and the "Market Peace"

Another important institution which is part of the marketplace is the "market peace." It is the function of the village-group where the market is situated to maintain the "peace of the market" thus assuring the safety of the traders. Ability to do this confers much prestige on the marketplace and attracts buyers and sellers. Usually this involves three integrated operations: ensuring that the weather is clement; that those who disturb the "market peace" are tried and punished without delay; that offenders who escape detection are hunted and punished by a "strong" market deity. The first operation involves the retention of a *dibia miri,* who "drives" rain from the local marketplace and "makes" it to disturb a rival one. (Rain making is an instrument of hostility among rival village-groups holding their market sessions on the same day.) The second operation involves the institutionalization of a "market" court whose officers police the marketplace and whose judges settle disputes arising between sellers and their customers. Finally, there is the market deity with an established reputation for killing undetected thieves who have been summoned before her.

Using the criteria of location and periodicity, we can distinguish two types of marketplace: the urban and the rural. The urban markets hold daily except Sundays. Since they are located in cities, their sanctions are provided by statutes. Except for a few farmers who sell their products either to the city middlemen or directly to the final consumers, the city traders are quite specialized, deriving the major source of their income from this occupation.

The rural markets differ in size and extent of their specialization. The most important ones are the rural weekly markets which hold every day in the Igbo four-day or eight-day week; the rural daily markets hold either in the morning or in the evening and include specialized markets whose transactions are restricted to one commodity, such as meat or palm liquor. Traditionally important but now in decay are the monthly rural fairs such as those held in Uzuakoli and Uburu.

The "Market Ring"

The important features of the rural markets are zoning, the absence of market fees, and a "market ring." Usually each marketplace is zoned into units selling one commodity, thus creating markets within a marketplace. The meat market, the cloth market, the food market, the palm liquor market, and the machine-goods markets are territorially distinguished by zoning. Unlike urban daily markets, rural markets do not normally charge market dues, and attract sellers by building shades for them. The trader, too, benefits from the fact that he can go from one marketplace in the ring to another without losing a trading day. The market ring has grown out of the fact that within each trading area it is possible to find an accessible market holding in each day of the four-day or eight-day Igbo week. An important feature of a market ring is a principal market on which other "feeder" markets depend. These latter may hold on the same day but late in the evening to allow the middlemen who attended the principal market to bring their commodities. Thus an industrious trader can attend two marketplaces in one day, buying from one and selling at the other. With the development of cities within what are traditional market ring areas, the city traders respond to the lure of the market ring. They bring their commodities and compete with the middlemen who buy in bulk from them in the city, thus creating the paradoxical situation in which the retail prices of certain machine-made goods may be lower in the principal rural markets than in the cities.

A Westerner visiting an Igbo rural market for the first time will be struck by three features of its operations: the commercial activities of women petty traders, the determination of prices, and the problem of defining who are wholesalers and who are retailers. He may, however, underestimate the role of the ubiquitous village or city trader locally known as the "Article Man."

Women dominate the retail trade. They are literally everywhere as buyers and sellers. Before marriage, girls are expected to acquire successful marketing techniques. Women are good bargain hunters. They haggle over prices in a manner which might frighten Westerners. They sell their husbands' as well as their own farm products: yams, palm oil, palm kernels, cassava, okra, melon, and "collected" products such as ọkazi, ọtazi, mushroom (ɛro), ọziza. Their traditional monopoly of commerce in cooked food has been challenged by those who serve food in the privacy of their huts, a service that attracts many customers. Many women engage in speculative trade, buying wholesale from distant traders (who must leave early) and selling in bulk and/or retail when the market is full. Shouts of *"Akara! Mayi-mayi! Dodo-kido!"* and so on, are heard from girls whose trays, well balanced on their heads, contain different types of machine-made goods, cakes, and cooked foods: *akara* (cassava or bean cake), *mayi-mayi* (cooked bean flour), *dodokido* (fried plantain); bottles of palm liquor, cube sugar, cigarettes, matches, and kola nuts. They have no shade as they parade the marketplace seeking customers for their wares.

When the market is over, it is through the women petty traders that goods reach the final customer in the village. A mother may need to buy salt or fish for the visitor who deserves "special" entertainment and who has dropped in without notice. She buys it from the local woman petty trader whose doors are always open when the market is over.

Price Determination

As in most West African markets, prices in the Igbo markets are determined by bargaining. Prices asked by sellers are always higher than those finally agreed upon. If the buyer considers the price too high, she shows her contempt by throwing the article down. Otherwise the usual procedure is for the buyer to handle the article, to show either approval or dissatisfaction while examining it, and then to offer a price normally lower than its worth. The seller may refuse to make a disadvantageous sale; the numerous competing sellers allow the buyer to try elsewhere. Other potential buyers for a given article may hang around waiting their turn. The actual buyer reserves the right to "show" a commodity to a neighbor before the price agreed upon is paid. A new development in city markets is to employ someone to offer inflated prices in order to confuse bona fide customers about prevailing prices.

Generally prices are set by supply and demand, a reflection of the relative scarcity of farm produce during the seasons of scarcity and plenty. As a result, prices of staples rise in the planting season and fall in the harvest season. The prices of machine-made goods are generally more stable and less erratic than those of farm products.

In the Igbo market economy, the "Article Man" deserves special treatment. He is a "new" trader, the creature of the machine-made goods and the demand for them. His operations make the distinction between a wholesaler and a retailer quite arbitrary. He fulfills both functions since he serves a wide range of clientele. Generally, he buys in small quantities from the city middlemen and retails in smaller quantities and sometimes in the smallest units. When he is the village barber, his shop becomes his marketplace. To the school children he provides pencils and pens, ink, paper, and textbooks; to the sick, he sells a wide range of medication from aspirin to penicillin drugs and hypodermic syringes—the latter two items going to a small trusted group who are the village "doctors."

The scale of the retail operations of these petty traders indicates the acute scarcity of capital and of spendable income. Matches are sold in boxes and in half-penny units; cigarettes are sold one by one; soap is sold in bars or in units costing a penny; envelopes sell in packets or four for a penny; writing pads of four sheets are a penny; kerosene is sold in amounts costing a penny to the price of a tin. From an article man one can buy almost anything that is machine-made provided there is a demand for it. By selling a wide range of goods the article man makes up in the number of his customers for what each customer lacks in purchasing power.

The credit system operating among the Igbo will be discussed in Chapter 9. It should, however, be mentioned here that farmers do not normally extend credit. They sell their produce for cash. But other traders, depending on the Club or Contribution system for their capital, extend short-term credit to trusted customers. The duration may vary from a whole market session (about eight to ten hours) to another market cycle falling at the next four-day or eight-day week. The greatest sanction for default is the fear of losing this privilege since no trader will want to deal with a delinquent customer-debtor.

Livestock Tenancy

If farming is the Igbo staff of life, trading their chief support and palm produce their cash earner, livestock tenancy is their source of prestige. It was mentioned earlier that the Igbo are very poor in livestock. Climatic conditions generally, and the tsetse fly in particular, limit the type of cows kept, and in recent times, the continued use of cassava as a semipermanent crop has led to the reduction of cows. Women oppose the keeping of cows because they destroy their cassava plants. Nevertheless, a few goats, sheep, poultry, pigs, and dogs are kept. They enter the agricultural cycle through the farmyard manure they provide. They are also an important source of wealth when sold for cash. Their demand for use in sacrifice is great.

Although livestock are normally acquired through open-market operations, most Igbo gain them first through a *contract of agistment* (livestock tenancy), even before they are old enough to earn money to buy an animal. A *contract of agistment* is defined as an agreement (verbal or written) under which an owner of livestock puts one or more animals under the charge of another person (chargee) to keep and nurture for the primary purpose of mutually sharing the increases or compensating the chargee (in lieu of increases) according to an agreed principle. To be executory, the contract must have a "material binder," that is, the animal must be transferred from the owner's custody to the chargee's. The promise to give an animal is not sufficient and does not create any *law of obligation* on the part of the promisor.

Livestock tenancy is fostered by an economic rationale that demands the spread of risks—in this case, domestic animals—among friends and relatives. Other factors are the demand for dogs by nursing mothers to take care of children's defecation, the tradition of "seeing" a child's new tooth with a hen, and the desire of travelers, especially the medicine men, to "buy" their way into new communities by the creation of livestock-tenant friends.

There are local variations in the sharing of animal increases, but general principles emerge. In regard to poultry, the principle is one of "equal sharing" of the increases—the pullets as well as the cockerels. The same principle is applied to goats, sheep, and dogs, though some communities adopt the ratio of two to one in favor of the owner. In the case of cows, the chargee's consideration is usually limited to a male and a female offspring, the owner claiming all other offspring. Even here local variations exist.

Since most Igbo do not keep all their livestock in their households, it becomes important to take note of this fact when estimating the wealth of the individual. This was not considered when the Colonial Administration, in its attempt to take a count of women's property, touched off the Women's Revolt in 1929.

Wage Labor

Farming, trading, local crafts, and livestock tenancy are no longer enough to maintain an adequate living standard for some Igbo. Many now seek wage labor. There is evidence that this is not a recent development, though the number of people involved has increased. The incidence of migrant labor is heaviest in the most densely populated areas. Territorial expansion—the traditional method of relieving population increase—was halted by the British intrusion into the country. With increasing population in the areas where population pressure had already become critical, there is a transition from a mainly agricultural to a predominantly trading-migrant economy: the areas of dense population coinciding with the areas of greatest petty trading and the supply of able-bodied migrants. These able-bodied migrants, who lack most industrial or technical skills and are forced to seek paid labor in the farms, factories, and other work places outside their homes, constitute a migrant labor force. It is not so much their absence from home as their temporary attachment to the labor force and to any particular job that are their distinguishing characteristics.

Using the criterion of the place of work, we can distinguish three categories of migrant labor among the Igbo: those who seek paid labor in Igboland, those who work in Nigeria but outside Igboland, and those who work outside Nigeria. The first category includes men and women. The men who lack sufficient good land for planting undertake wage labor for others in less densely populated agricultural areas. Formerly this labor was paid in kind, seed yams being the form of payment. Oguta, Ikwerre, Ngwa, Ndoki, and Bende are among the most important centers for this kind of labor. The work, which is agricultural, is mainly seasonal, labor being mostly demanded during such farm operations as bush clearing, hoeing, planting, and staking.

Women are usually engaged to weed the farm or to plant cassava and cocoyams for others who aspire to take the cocoyam title. They are away for only a short time, and this kind of labor attracts widows and old women more than the young ones, who tend to engage in petty trading instead. Some women may be engaged to crack palm kernels for other women whose trading activities do not permit them to do the work. A recent development is the opportunity offered to women by the installation of the Pioneer Oil Mills where women pick palm kernels for wages.

The opportunities offered to labor, skilled and unskilled, by the economic developments taking place in Nigeria in the last forty years have been grasped by the Igbo. The growing cities, the expanding road construction, the building boom, the new industries, and the oil explorations are creating job opportunities demanding varying degrees of skills. At every level, the Igbo are found. Besides these new opportunities, the Igbo provide some of the farm labor in other non-Igbo areas in Southern Nigeria. The rubber plantations of the Midwest and the cocoa farms of the Yoruba may be mentioned in this respect. Exploiting the opportunity offered by the scarcity of machine-made goods during and immediately after World War II, many Igbo became itinerant tinkers, repairing broken iron pots and plates; fashioning new buckets, cooking pots, cymbals for school bands, and households utensils from old zinc sheets, kerosene tins, and gasoline drums. This occupation, is still an important source of livelihood for some Igbo.

Nigeria is not yet able to absorb all its unskilled labor. There is thus an attraction for some Igbo to seek paid labor outside the country. Cameroon, the island of Fernando-Po, Gabon, and Ghana have Nigerian migrants who are predominantly Igbo.

Unfortunately there is no published study from which quantitative data on this problem can be drawn. A serious drawback to regional comparison is that migrant labor is either undefined or vaguely defined to include such character-istics as the temporary attachment to the labor force and the absence from home, which are also among some of the characteristics of skilled and semiskilled and even expatriate labor. In her five sample censuses taken at Mbaise, Shirley Arden-er reports that "the average proportion of the population living abroad was ap-proximately 16%" (1953:128). This type of information does not help us to distinguish between the categories of people involved. It is true that Mbaise is facing a serious pressure on land; and equally true that it has many skilled men occupying responsible positions in government, education, and industry. Normal-ly, these people must live and work away from home since most Igbo areas are predominantly rural. We still do not have a quantitative picture of the migrant population in this or any other area.

There is no single way in which the Igbo earn their living. For most peo-ple, agriculture is the principal means and may long continue to be so. For others, there is a flight from the land—a flight due not to disdain or disrespect but to the poor returns it offers. Those who cling to the land must supplement their earnings from other sources: trading, paid labor, livestock tenancy, handi-craft, and palm produce. The educated Igbo have entered the professions and white-collar jobs; others are successful businessmen. Although politics is creating a new "industry," law, medicine, education, and business administration provide a livelihood for Igbo professional people and these frontiers are rapidly increas-ing.

3

Helping the Town "To Get Up"

"And how often does one hear:

"We want to make our place—or our market—get up" (Green 1947: 255). This kind of sentiment, which the people of the village-group (town) of Agbaja in southern Okigwi District expressed to Miss Green, an anthropologist, who worked among them, is a common theme in Igbo social life. "To get up" is a sentiment which nourishes community spirit; the fruit of the latter is community development. To belong to a forward-looking town is a source of pride to the villager and the "son abroad"; to suggest how a town can "get up" and to help it to realize this goal is to be a good citizen, a man of great prestige, *okwu omɛɛ*—"One who says and does what he says."

Community spirit is very strong among the Igbo. Almost from the first the individual is aware of his dependence on his kin group and his community. He also realizes the necessity of making his own contribution to the group to which he owes so much. He seldom, if ever, becomes really detached from that group, wherever he may live. His concern for the progress of his town makes him loyal to it. It is his ultimate desire to return to his village after earning money elsewhere. To him, the village is the appropriate place for retirement; the city, a place to earn money. Thus it is only by contributing to the progress of his town and increasing its prestige that his own feeling of security is enhanced.

Earlier Patterns of "Getting Up"

In the days before contact with Europeans the prestige and influence of a town was measured by the strength of its able-bodied warriors, its diplomacy in dealing with its neighbors, its access to long-distance trade routes, the power of its oracles, the importance of its marketplace, and the degree of its craft specialization.

Among the Igbo village-groups which achieved fame for their war-making power were the Edda and the Abam. These groups have a strong age-grade organization which required the taking of an enemy's head as a precondition for manly status. Every year their uninitiated youth terrorized their neighbors while hunting for heads. When the slave trade became lucrative, the Aro people employed the Edda and the Abam as mercenaries. The military operations of the latter earned them as much infamy as it earned the Aro prestige.

Although the power of the Edda and the Abam rested on military might, that of the Aro, Umunoha, Awka, and Ozuzu rested on their oracles, erroneously termed by the British "jujus." We shall hear more about these oracles in Chapter 11. In the present context we are discussing them as the main source of the influence of the towns which controlled them. In their time these oracles—the *Ibini Ɔkpabɛ* of Aro-Chukwu, the *Igwɛka-Ala* of Umunoha, the *Agbala* of Awka, and the *Amadi Ɔha* or *Kamalu* of Ozuzu—were the most powerful legal institutions in Igboland and served as the highest court of appeal. Until the Euro-American slave trade their influence seemed rather regional, each oracle serving the social, religious, and political needs of the village-groups nearest it. Except for the *Ibini Ɔkapabɛ,* other oracles on the other side of the Imo River could be installed at a fee for villages which wanted them. It was the impact of the slave trade and the strategic location of the *Ibini Ɔkpabɛ* (on an island commanding access to the sea and protected by a shallow gorge accessible only by a narrow, tortuous bush path) that made it the premier oracle in the last century. The prestige which the oracle gave to the Aro people was such that "the blood of an Aro man was [regarded as] too precious to be spilt in battle and his death would call for large scale reprisals which were avoided whenever possible as unnecessary and wasteful" (Basden 1938:385).

Although the prestige bestowed by the oracles died with British contact and the pacification of Igboland, marketplaces have managed to retain their status and prestige. It is true that some markets have declined in importance while others have prospered as the result of the changes in the location of roads and the shifts in population. Onitsha market is an example of the latter, whereas Uburu and Uzuakoli markets are examples of the former. The prestige of Onitsha is derived from many factors. It is an educational as well as a religious center; moreover, its marketplace, built at a cost of nearly two million dollars, is probably the best in West Africa. The early introduction of a Western type of education gives Onitsha the heaviest concentration of educated men and women in Igboland. In the eyes of most Igbo, Onitsha is a model of a town "which has gotten up."

Uburu and Uzuakoli, ancient Igbo marketplaces, have not had the luck of Onitsha. About twenty-one miles northwest of Afikpo is Uburu, once the only inland salt center of Igboland. Its prestige was built on salt; its decline followed the cheap importation of salt from Europe. In pre-British days, all trade routes led to the Uburu market. It was a meeting place for the Igbo world of those days. Holding a monopoly in the supply of salt, which only their naked women worked from their salt lake, Uburu also became a slave market and a market for horses, cows, and anything else brought in by traders.

Agbagwu, the great fair at Uzuakoli which held an eight-day session in its monthly cycle, conferred much prestige on Uzuakoli. My elderly Igbo informants described the former importance of Uburu and Uzuakoli: "You could buy anything in those markets." This statement is no longer true. For one thing, they are no longer slave markets; for another, their commercial importance has suffered because of the changes in the character of the goods demanded by consumers—goods the markets are unable to offer.

Today there is an important shift in what is necessary to make a town "get up." There is consensus among the Igbo that education is the key to "progress" as it is now reinterpreted. The educational progress of Igboland owes much to the missionaries, for there are few Igbo leaders today who did not attend the mission schools. On the other hand, the success of the missionaries was in no small part due to the cooperation and the community spirit of the people among whom they worked. To today's Igbo, schools, colleges, maternity centers, and hospitals are the new symbols of progress. It is not so much access to these facilities as their physical presence in the village for which the people strive. A village which aspires "to get up" must acquire these new symbols of status within its fence. They represent community development, the result of voluntary community action for which the Igbo are noted.

Modern Development and Self-Help

Community development depends on self-help. The Igbo know this. They are prepared to make the sacrifice which self-help demands provided they can point to its fruit as their own. The Colonial Administration became increasingly aware of this trait in Igbo character when the people began to question the wisdom of locating all the new improvements—hospitals, maternity centers, schools, and council halls—at the administrative capitals. They wanted these facilities inside each village. Their concentration in one center is as much opposed by the Igbo as the concentration of political power in the hands of one individual. In the eyes of the Colonial Administration, following "the Igbo Way" was an economic waste; to the people, the physical presence of these facilities is a source of prestige for which they are prepared to pay in labor, materials, and money. This they did—and are still doing. There is no Igbo village today which cannot point with pride to a motor road, water points, a marketplace, a village school, a maternity center, or a village hall, or even a combination of these as the result of their own efforts. The modern symbols of intervillage rivalry, they provide the community which owns them something to boast about. Those who are not organized effectively enough to achieve these goals are constantly reminded by their leaders that they have become an object of derision. Their struggle to catch up stimulates in more successful villages the desire to remain on top.

"Human Investment"

The modern pattern of intervillage competition is not limited to rivalry for the possession of roads, marketplaces, schools, and village halls. The struggle for political independence brought the realization that leaders educated in the Western tradition were necessary to success in "getting up." Thus the emphasis was shifted to "human investment"—the training of the modern elite. The prestige of *Nwa jere Oyibo*—the son who was educated in white man's country—is not merely a personal one. It is shared by the whole village. The drive for university scholarships for the deserving sons and daughters became as infectious as the drive for schools and council halls. The "sons abroad" (as the Igbo who live in cities are called and call themselves) encouraged the idea among the people at home. There is a common refrain in the Village Family Meetings or Progressive Unions: "It is a matter of shame that we have educated nobody abroad. Other towns are ahead of us and we shall soon be their slaves. We can no longer content ourselves with 'equal heads.' We must have 'educated heads'—'the mouths that can speak for us.' "

This program of human investment has two facets. At the individual level, it gives much prestige; in fact, a man who can afford it (but few can, because for most Igbo, it is a great personal sacrifice) is expected to give his brothers and half brothers at least a high school education. At the community level, the "home" resources (i.e., the harvest of oil palms) are taxed and "abroad" a cash levy is paid by city dwellers in order to help at least one person to receive a university education. The individual who is a beneficiary of such a scholarship program is expected to make a later contribution to the welfare of his town. This may take the form of a donation to the town scholarship fund, a contribution to other welfare projects, or the sponsorship of other students. His home town boys expect him to help them get work in the city and even to put them up while they are searching for it. To the American, this social pressure to support relatives and friends and share with them one's resources may seem to have a strong "leveling effect," but the Igbo see it otherwise. For them it is a way of helping others "to get up."

The willingness to help less fortunate people get adjusted to new situations is not a recent development. Even in the slave plantations of the New World, Igbo slaves helped their newly arrived countrymen to adjust themselves. In Haiti, where the conditions of slavery made for great African retentions, the same pattern was followed. "The Ibos," we are told, "were found excellent for work in the fields, yet difficult to manage. . . . Nonetheless, many slaves from this tribe were acquired. Their strong communal and tribal ties made it advantageous for those who owned them to obtain more of them, since newcomers were accorded help, care and instructions by those who had preceded them" (Herskovits 1937:20–21).

The Improvement Unions

In Nigerian and other west African cities where some Igbo work or seek paid labor, the need to protect themselves and to educate the newcomers in the city ways, as well as to act as pressure groups in their respective village and district politics, led to the formation of various associations called Family Meetings or Improvement Unions. These associations meet at home once or twice a year (at Easter and/or Christmas) to plan welfare developments, map strategy for the local councilors, and, in an election year, influence voting through propaganda and the reinterpretation of major political issues in language their people can understand. As opinion leaders and innovators their role is to explain the demands of their changing world to their people and to analyze the implications of the political choices they make at the polls.

The "sons abroad," who make up the various Family Meetings, Town and Divisional Improvement Unions, form the core of Igbo educated elite. Except for teachers, nurses, and the local government personnel, the village has little employment opportunity for other categories of educated men and women. This helps to explain the attention given to the "sons abroad" when they give their opinion on local politics and its trends. For the mass of the people, good government is synonymous with good roads, schools, maternity homes, and post offices. It is around these that local and national politics revolve. For the masses, the politics of village development is the only important politics. But it is often a development they must pay for in addition to their taxes. That this does not seem to matter the following case illustrates. A postal agency in one Ngwa village-group was temporarily shut down following what the Post and Telegraph Department called an "irregularity" on the part of the local agent. A rival village, one mile away, seized this opportunity to apply for the relocation of this agency in its village. When official permission was refused, the people decided to rent a postal mail bag from the nearest post office, which is nine miles away, even though the disputed postal agency had been reopened and another postal agency is three miles away. To an American, this may appear a fuss over nothing; to the Igbo, it is anything but that. The American sees a post office as a place that handles ingoing and outgoing mail; the Igbo thinks of the post office as a symbol of status which its presence confers on his village or town.

For the Igbo, helping the town "to get up" is nothing short of an obsession. It requires community action and self-sponsored welfare programs, which in turn demand sacrifice from the individual as well as from the town. The town helps its citizens to "get up" just as the citizens help the town. The prestige of one is tied to the prestige of the other. Igbo receptivity to change and their separatism cannot be understood if we do not take their concept of "getting up" into consideration.

4

Igbo Ways in Government

HE POLITICAL INSTITUTIONS in Igboland differ in their structure. Some of these, like the kingship institutions of Onitsha, Nri, and Aguleri, are intrusive traits. Although age-grade associations, title-making societies, *Dibia* fraternities (medicine men), secret societies, and oracles[1] are among the traditional instruments of government, the role of each in the political processes of a given village-group differs markedly. Nevertheless, there emerges a general pattern of political process which is shared by all Igbo.

As a first orientation, we may distinguish two layers of political structure: the village and the village-group. At the village level of government (this varies in size and population), the accepted practice is a direct democracy, a system which has survived the British contact. At the village-group level, a representative system is adopted; equality among the associating villages is maintained through the principle of equal "sharing of kola" and equal contribution of material resources needed for the survival of the group. The varying internal segmentation of each village does not change the principle of equality among the village-group.

Each village is autonomous and "sovereign" in most matters affecting it. What may modify this sovereignty is the "charter," the myth from which the village-group derives its solidarity. The village is further segmented into a number of lineages and each lineage into major and minor sublineages.

Authority in the "Family"

Each lineage is made up of a number of territorially kin-based units called *ǝmǝnna*—a fluid term whose narrowest referent is the children of the

---

[1] Igbo oracles are deities and are sometimes powerful spirits which have been institutionalized by a community to serve as a medium by which hidden knowledge and divine will might be ascertained. For more details, see Chapter 11.

same father but of different mothers; its widest referent is the patrilineal members, real or putative,[2] whom one cannot marry. Sometimes it is loosely applied to all the members of the village-group in contradistinction to other like village-groups. In terms of residence, ǝmǝnna is made up of a number of compounds. It is in these compounds that traditional authority mainly lies.

The compound (ɛzi, obi) consists of a number of economically independent households each with a man or a woman as the householder. All the householders and their dependents recognize the authority of the compound head and would not make a major political decision without first consulting with him. Onyɛ nwɛ ɛzi (obi), as the compound head is called, has numerous ritual, moral, and legal rights and obligations. He offers sacrifice for the welfare of his compound members, whom he helps to extricate from their ritual, social, and legal problems; he settles the numerous matrimonial cases and confers a special name on each child born in his compound. In Igbo idiom, he is the "eyes of his compound members as they are his ears." He represents them in their external dealings with other like social groups. Any injury inflicted on any member of his group without his having been first notified is considered a personal injury for which he makes a personal reprisal if need be. In effect, a strong compound head is a shield of protection and the wall or fence surrounding his compound is his group's castle.

In return, the compound head receives respect, obedience, and material tokens of goodwill. Formerly he was entitled to oriɛ-day work; this means that in the farming season, members of his compound worked on his field for one day of the Igbo four-day or eight-day week, depending on the locality. Today he may receive from his "sons abroad" a head of tobacco, some machetes, files, and money to hire labor although those at home may ignore him. Where the compound head is ɔkpara (ɔpara), he is entitled to receive, on oriɛ days, the palm or raphia liquor tapped for his compound members. Such liquor is not sold; it is drunk in obu, ovu (his lounge) by all who happen to be present. In those communities where the ɔfɔ-land survives (land tied to the ritual office of ɔkpara, head of a sublineage) he alone exercises usufructuary rights over it when he happens to be the ɔfɔ-holder of his lineage segment.

At a higher level than the compound units we have the lineage,[3] whose most important ritual figure is the ɔkpara. He holds the lineage ɔfɔ, which is very important in Igbo political processes. Though a compound head in his own right, his role as the lineage head is a unique one. He may be the oldest member of the lineage or the oldest member of the senior segment of the lineage. Though every male head of each sublineage is termed ɔkpara, the most important person in this context is the lineage head. He derives his authority from the fact that he is regarded as the intermediary between his lineage and the ancestors. His authority symbol, ɔfɔ, is a branch of the tree known as

---

[2] A kinship tie and behavior accorded to a person for whom a vague relationship is supposed to exist or to have existed may be called a *putative* kinship.

[3] A lineage is a consanguineal (blood-related) kin group consisting of all the descendants in one line (either male or female only) of a named individual through a number of generations. Most Igbo communities reckon descent through the male line. The social group they call ǝmǝnna is what anthropologists call a *patrilineage*.

Detarium elastica. This should not be confused with personal *ɔfɔ* of the priests and the medicine men. The latter is the symbol of priesthood; the former, a symbol of ritual authority. The *ɔkpara* wields both.

The priestly function of the *ɔkpara* includes sacrificing to the earth deity (*Ala*) on behalf of all the members of the lineage. His political power is limited, being essentially presidential in nature. He simply presides over the meetings in which disputes may be referred for arbitration. He does not normally initiate political action, but is always aware of what action is planned, for he must give his opinion on their conflict with custom and tradition. He cannot interfere in the internal affairs of the component lineage segments. His power to punish is limited to one sanction: cursing people on his *ɔfɔ*—a sanction often threatened but very seldom invoked. The office of the *ɔkpara* carries much responsibility and this calls for restraint on his part even when personally he is wronged.

Succession to the office of *ɔkpara* follows the adelphic principle, passing from the incumbent to his next brother in line rather than from father to son. Even in this case, it is not an automatic succession. Character is the overriding factor, and a candidate qualified by the age-order principle may be turned down because he is considered to have a questionable character. Although character is important for election or selection for office, the personality of the officeholder determines how effective the office will be.

Autonomy of the Village

Government at the village level is an exercise in direct democracy. It involves all the lineages and requires the political participation of all the male adults. Though it forms part of the village-group, the widest political community, the village is autonomous in its affairs and accepts no interference or dictation from any other group. The institutions which are utilized in the political processes of the village include *Amala, Ɔha* (a general assembly), the title-making societies, the *Dibia* fraternity (a priestly association), the secret society, oracles, and the age-grade associations. Leadership is provided by the *ɔfɔ*-holders, the titled men and women of wealth who have risen spontaneously in the village and have developed their power and influence gradually.

Legislative activities are performed by all adult males meeting in *ad hoc* general assembly called the *Amala* or *Ɔha*. The meeting place may be in an open square where all the paths of the village converge. In modern times, a more permanent building, the village hall, has become common. Public matters are thrown open for discussion. Every villager who can contribute to the discussion is given a hearing. When the matter has been thoroughly talked out, the leaders from each lineage in the village retire for *izuzu* (consultation). The right to participate in *izuzu* is a greatly cherished and respected one and is restricted to men of weight and prestige, men who have the wisdom to understand and appreciate all schools of thought and achieve a compromise which the *Amala* can accept. After *izuzu,* a spokesman who is chosen not because of his age but for his power of oratory, his persuasive talents, and his ability to put the verdict in perspective, announces the decision. This is either accepted by the *Amala* by general acclamation or rejected by shouts of derision. In the latter event the view of the assembly prevails. The Igbo are jealous of their legislative authority and are not willing to surrender it to a small group of individuals.

Once a decision has been thus acclaimed into law, it is given a "ritual binder" by the *ɔfɔ* holders, who invoke this formula: "This *iwu* [law] is in accordance with our custom and must be obeyed and respected. Those who refuse to obey the law, may *ɔfɔ* kill them." Each time the *ɔfɔ* is struck on the ground (usually four times), the assembly assents with *"iha"* ("Let it be so"). This done, it becomes the duty of each adult male and householder to explain the legislation to his household group and to see to it that the members respect the law.

Matters within the legislative competence of the village formerly ranged from the control and regulation of economic affairs to questions of war, peace, and defense. The economic control exercised by the village may take the form of boycotting an enemy market, regulating the firing of bush, setting the price of palm liquor demanded in the village, or levying taxes to pay for the welfare schemes initiated by the village.

The village assembly is concerned not only with deliberative and legislative functions; it also deals with judicial, administrative, and executive matters. There is no separation of powers involved. The village, whether its members are assembled after a funeral rite, a path clearing, or for some other purpose, is an all-purpose governmental machinery. The people who make the laws also interpret and execute them. When it meets, the village assembly may make new laws, try old cases, or delegate its executive powers to a group of age-grades for action.

The legal procedure followed does not involve rigid division between civil and criminal offenses. Rather, the Igbo make a distinction between those offenses which are *nsɔ* or *alɵ*—are abomination—and those which are not. The former include incest and homicide. Incest is defined as "sexual intercourse with a person one cannot marry." It requires ritual purification. Where it was mother-son incest or sister-brother incest, the people involved were sold into slavery. Otherwise adultery is a personal injury for which the adulterer might be assaulted or be asked to pay compensation, or the injured husband might choose to violate with impunity women belonging to the adulterer's group.

Homicide is an offense against *ala*—the earth deity. If a villager is involved, the murderer is expected to hang himself, after which the *ɵmɵ ɔkpɵ* (daughters of the village) perform the rite of *izafu utɵ ɔchɵ*—sweeping away the ashes of murder. If the murderer has fled, his extended family must also flee, and the property of all is subject to raids. When the murderer is eventually caught, he is required to hang himself to enable the *ɵmɵ ɔkpɵ* to perform their rites. It is important to realize that the village has no power to impose capital punishment. In fact, no social group or institution has this power. Everything affecting the life of the villager is regulated by custom. The life of the individual is highly respected; it is protected by the earth-goddess. The villagers can bring social pressure, but the murderer must hang himself.

The treatment of a thief varies with the nature of the theft, and whether it affects the villagers or outsiders. Stealing among kinsmen calls for a warning for the first offense if what was stolen was a trifle. Otherwise the offender is tied up for days without food; if caught red-handed he is carried about the village with the stolen property conspicuously exhibited, while passers-by curse, ridicule, and spit on him. Stealing from outsiders is a more serious matter. The thief is held until a substantial ransom is paid by his relatives. This is considered a favored treatment which is subject to reciprocity. When this reciprocity is absent, the thief could be sold by his captors. If the thief is not actually caught and the evidence against a suspect is not convincing, the suspect is made to swear an oath. If he is a notorious character, he is made to provide "oath helpers" (in Igbo idiom, people who support his back). Should his kinsmen refuse to be "oath helpers," this fact is enough to convict of theft. If he swears his oath and no bad luck befalls him within one year, his *iŋə ishi* (innocence) is regarded as proved and he celebrates it appropriately.

Under a constitution like that of the Igbo, which does not provide for a specialized court, judicial matters are *ad hoc* affairs. The injured party takes the initiative. He may appeal to the head of the compound of the offender or to a body of arbitrators.

Since the arbitrators have no means of enforcing their decision, for it to be respected it must be acceptable to both parties. If this fails, the injured party may beat the village drum to summon the *Amala*. The special friends of the litigants are invited to help resolve the matter. Other institutions which may be appealed to for a judicial opinion include the age-grade society, the *Dibia* fraternity, various title-making societies, and the *ɔkɔnkɔ* society.

Jurisdiction may be taken away from human tribunals and given to such supernatural tribunals as the oracles. The last court of appeal, they are used when all the tribunals of the land fail to give the litigants satisfaction.

The executive function of the village is vested in the youth through their age-grade organization. Besides serving as a social indicator which separates the seniors from the juniors, the age-grade association is a means of allocating public duties, guarding public morality through the censorship of members' behavior, and providing companionship and mutual insurance for members. It is to them that the police functions of the village are delegated. They collect levies, keep surveillance over the property of the village, and run its errands. The money they collect is usually locked up in the village treasury. The village treasurer (a new office which came with the money economy) is chosen primarily for his integrity. He is not selected from the lineage which fills the office of the "key holder." Before these offices were created, the normal procedure was to raise money by *ad hoc* collection as the need arose.

Government of the Village-Group (Town)

Although village government is based on direct democracy, the government of the village-group involves a representative principle; the political solidarity and autonomy of the former contrast with the tenuous political relationship and "minimal" government characteristic of the latter. The village-group government is neither a federation nor a confederation. It has no well-defined powers except on matters affecting the earth-goddess and the common marketplaces. What laws or decisions it makes are not binding on any village which is not represented or which disagrees with the others. The power of the village-group is based not on the possession of a standing or *ad hoc* army, nor on any admitted right to use coercion, but rather on the consensus of the villages. In the assembly, every village has equal voice. There is no majority decision. The village representatives are not a permanent body of legislators but are selected at each session for their ability to present the point of view of their village. They have a "delegate" and not a "representative" status and cannot commit their village to any matter not previously discussed and agreed upon by it. The association imposes equal labor and money contributions on all the member villages, obligations compensated by the principle of equal sharing of facilities and perquisites.

In recent years, the village-group (the town) has grown in importance. The literate Igbo who work away from the village have realized the need for a wider political community. The drive for a "welfare town," in which schools, hospitals, colleges, good roads, and a rural water supply form part of the "village-group complex," has led to the Igbo's increasing emphasis on his town. These facilities which no single village can supply unaided, but cooperation at the village-group level makes them possible.

Following this discussion of the principles of Igbo government we shall see how they are applied in three different settings—Onitsha, Agbaja in Okigwi, and Aro-Chukwu.

Three Sample Governments

Onitsha is a town on the Niger. Its people claim descent from Chima, an eponymous ancestor who came into their present territory from Benin. Their village-group, which first consisted of two main divisions (Umuezechima and Ugwunabonkpo), has since segmented into six villages.

Obi is the official title of the king of Onitsha. His prime minister is called Ꝉnowu. Below the *Obi* are three colleges of titled men called *Ndichiε: Ndichiε Umε, Ndichiε Ꝉkwa,* and *Ndichiε Ꝉkwa-Aranzε.* Each college has a hierarchy of officials who achieved their present status by taking a costly ꝈzꝈ title.

Adult males are organized into age-grade and age-set associations from which the *Ndichiε* draw men who perform police functions in their respective villages. In theory, the government of Onitsha consists of the *Obi* and his

Ndichiɛ Umɛ, but in practice, each village has a large measure of local autonomy. The rights of the *Obi* and his council are regulated by custom. When
they exceed their rights, the offended village boycotts the *Obi's* palace. Each
Ndichiɛ holds his own village court, presides over the government of his village, leads his men to the king's war, may act as the king's ambassador, and
represents the interests of his village in the king's council.

The office of the *Obi* is elective and not hereditary. It is vested in the
Umuezechima group of villages (Umudɛi, Umuɛzɛaroli, and Obiokporo),
each of which, in theory, has a right to take office, probably in rotation. "In
fact, Obiokporo has never had an *Obi* and the office has tended to remain in
the same ward [village], most of the nineteenth-century *Obi's,* for example,
coming from Umuezearoli" (Jones, 1956:28). This "manipulation" of the
elective principle has made succession to the office of *Obi* a hotly disputed one in
recent years.

Constitutional monarchy is intrusive in Igboland. The Onitsha traditional
system of government therefore contrasts with other systems. In the village-
group of Agbaja (about sixty-five miles east of Onitsha), for instance, the
eleven villages manifest the same "dual organization" as that in Onitsha—
seven villages in Agbaja Ama and four in Agbaja Owɛrɛ.

According to their mythical charter, the people of Agbaja claim descent
from Ngalaba and his wife *Ɔkpɵ Itɛ,* both of whom were created there and
once lived on the spot where their marketplace is situated. Ngalaba and his
wife had eleven sons, each of whom founded one of the eleven villages. The
village of the eldest son holds the big *ɔfɔ,* a position which gives it a ritual
precedence over others but no authority roles.

Umuɛkɛ, one of the villages in Agbaja, is autonomous in its affairs. The
villagers make their laws, try their cases, and punish offenders. The only higher
authority appealed is the oracle. The appeal is made when there is some
difficulty or uncertainty, or when the offender is unknown or the evidence is
scanty. The solidarity of Agbaja as a village-group is explained by their
common territoriality, their mythical charter, and their possession of a common guardian deity as well as a central marketplace.

The constitution of Aro-Chukwu is similar to that of Agbaja. The people
of Arochukwu occupy a territory about twenty-five square miles, approximately
nineteen miles from the eastern bank of Cross River. They achieved notoriety
because of their oracle, *Ibini Ɔkpabɛ,* which became an instrument of exploita-
tion among the Igbo communities in their sphere of influence. Their power
grew, thanks to their manipulation of this oracle for their own ends and to
their depredations, which were furthered by the employment of such head-
hunting mercenaries as the Abam, Abiriba, Edda, and Ɔhafia.

The early history of the Aro is obscure. Tradition claims that they grew
from two village-groups, Amuze and Ibom Isi, to nine, the process of segmentation resulting in the present nineteen villages in Aro-Chukwu. Matters of
common interest to these nineteen villages are discussed in a general assembly
in which each is represented. No village "could be bound by a law or decision
made at a meeting in the absence of its representative" (Jones 1956:5). The

principle of equal sharing of rights and privileges is sacred. To be effective decisions must be unanimous, since there is no sanction strong enough to coerce any dissenting member into submission.

The ɛzɛ of Aro (chief) has only a presidential function at the meetings of the nineteen villages. Although young men are allowed a voice, the government of the nineteen is dominated by "elders" from each village because of the need to keep the manipulation of the oracle secret.

At the village level, Aro government is a direct democracy. The affairs of the village are decided by a general assembly in which men and women can participate. However, effective control is in the hands of elders, members of an age set whose turn it is to govern the village at a particular period in their age-grade cycle.

The picture of the Igbo political community which emerges from these settings is one that is territorially small enough to make direct democracy possible at the village level as well as representative assembly at the village-group level; a government in which the principle of equality is respected; in which the use of force is minimal or absent; and in which there are leaders rather than rulers, and political cohesion is achieved by rules rather than by laws and by consensus rather than by dictation. In general, the Igbo have not achieved any political structure which can be called a federation, a confederacy, or a state.

Igboland under Colonial Rule

The British Colonial Administration, which took over control of Igboland in the first decade of this century, did not understand the traditional political institutions of the people. Failing to find powerful chiefs who wielded influence over a large territory, as were found in the northern and western parts of Nigeria, they naïvely concluded that the Igbo were living in "ordered anarchy." Without considering its implications, they imposed a system of direct administration on the Igbo.

THE DIRECT ADMINISTRATION   The direct administration had two important features: It based the Colonial Administration of Igboland on all-purpose native courts, which were established by the Native Courts Proclamation (1900) and derived their revenue from indirect taxation. Following the Proclamation Igboland was arbitrarily carved into Native Court Areas, formed by grouping together a number of contiguous village-groups which were traditionally sovereign political units. Each Court Area constituted a native court system, an all-purpose administrative machinery. The British district commissioner was the president of the court; other personnel included warrant chiefs, the court clerk, and the court messengers.

THE WARRANT CHIEFS   The warrant chiefs, hand-picked by the district commissioner, were believed by him to represent the village-groups in the court area. They were given a cap of office and a warrant of authority which was backed by the coercive force of the administration. The people who were appointed warrant chiefs were "those who impressed the District Commissioner with their courage to come forward and meet the Europeans. The traditional rulers seldom passed this test, and so were, for the most part, left out" (Nwabueze, 1963:70). Although the warrant chiefs held judgeships in these courts, their actual role was that of mere advisers whose opinion was sought by the president (a white administrator) when he needed assistance on some points of customary law.

Among the important innovations of the court system were the provision made for prisons and the office of court clerk. The court clerk kept a record of the court's decisions and supervised the court messengers, who executed such court duties as serving summonses, maintaining order in court, and making arrests. The decisions of the courts were subject to review on appeal.

The difficulties in the direct administration program became clear with the passage of time. The warrant chiefs were not in any way representative of the village-groups they were supposed to serve. Most of them were "new men" who had no status in society; if they had any claim to leadership, it was confined to their extended family. Reforms came in 1918, when the Native Court Ordinance (No. 5 as amended to 1922) abolished the office of district commissioner in the native courts and thus made the courts really "native." Nevertheless this reform created many other problems. The withdrawal of the district commissioners (they were now called district officers) gave the warrant chiefs an opportunity to abuse their powers. They became more corrupt, some even holding their own private courts. The unsuccessful party at the private courts of the warrant chiefs was even more unsuccessful when he submitted the matter to the native court. The court clerk, the only semiliterate member of the court system, usurped the power of the former district commissioner and became as corrupt as the warrant chiefs, using the improvised prison under his control to further his own designs.

In 1928 the adult males were directly taxed for the first time and the Native Treasury was added to the Native Court complex. The following year, Okugo, a warrant chief from Oloko, touched off a massive protest of Igbo women when he attempted to assess their property in his area. The association of taxation with the assessment of wealth was a logical one. Before their taxation in 1928, the property of the men had been assessed in 1927. What other reason could justify the assessment of women's property, the women reasoned, unless a plan to tax them was in the offing? This mishandled protest (called the Aba Riots in Government reports), which left thirty-two women dead and dying and thirty-one wounded, dramatically revealed the problems and the weaknesses of the administrative system. The reorganizations (1930–1931) which followed from the Reports of the two Commissions of Enquiry investigating the Aba Riots, as well as the immediate anthropological investigations, which were granted top priority, showed the administration's concern over correcting the wrongs of the previous three decades.

THE REFORMS OF 1930–1931   The new native courts which came with indirect rule were adapted to the existing institutions. Their zones were small, thus reflecting the nature of the social groupings. The number of benches or judgeships was increased. "Warrants" were given to social units, such as villages, instead of to individuals. The villages selected court judges to represent them. The degree of flexibility allowed was such that some courts either selected presidents for each sitting or had no presidents at all. The powers of the court clerks and the court messengers were checked by the district officers. At least two major problems were created by the new system: "massed benches" contained up to sixty or more judges in some places; the personnel of the court judges were constantly changing because of the rotating judgeship among members of a social grouping holding a common warrant. The judicial changes which came into effect in 1945 made it possible to reduce the size of the "massed benches"; achieve a stable court judgeship through consultation, selection, or election; and evolve a system of "a panel with rotating benches." In this system a full panel of judges, consisting of about fifteen to twenty-one members, may be divided into three benches with five to seven members on the panel sitting in rotation.

Changes Preceding Independence

Some minor changes have been made in this system recently. The term "Customary Courts" has replaced "Native Courts." District and county courts have been created from the existing courts, thus abolishing some of them. Literacy qualifications have eliminated some judges from the panel, and the presidents of the district and the county courts are appointed by the Minister of Local Government.

A system of local government based on a three-tier model—urban, district, and local councils—(two tiers in rural areas), came into operation in 1948. The majority of the councilors are elected, but a few traditional rulers take part in these councils wherever their status justifies it. The control of council affairs rests with the elected members. Although these councils have produced a higher political integration, they have not replaced the traditional village-group government.

$\boxed{5}$

Founding a New Family

A MONG THE IGBO married life is the normal condition for both men and women; polygyny,[1] a symbol of high social status, is the ideal. However, the great majority of Igbo marriages are monogamous, reflecting, on the one hand, the force of economic circumstances and, on the other, the new tendency of the literate professional and "white-collar" class to acquire modern status symbols (thus cars are replacing plural wives as status symbols) and to conform to the norms of their Christian faith. In the Igbo marriage, we are interested in the process by which a new family is created, in the acquisition of reciprocal rights and duties of a couple, and in the manner in which the status of the children of the union is guaranteed.

Emphasis on Married Status

Some of the rules which govern Igbo marriage are based on the Igbo status system. Marriage between *osu* (cult slave) and *diala* (freeborn) is taboo. Endogamy, which prohibits marriage outside one's own social group, exists only in one form: *osu* must marry among their own social group. In their respective communities, both *osu* and *diala* obey the rules of exogamy by marrying outside their local groups. Lineage exogamy is the rule. Furthermore, a person may not marry within the segment of his or her mother's or father's mother's patrilineage. The purpose of the initial inquiry conducted by families at the earliest point of the marriage negotiation is to ensure that this rule is not broken. There are no preferential marriages and no father-in-law or mother-in-law avoidances. Marriages between slaves and free men were allowed.

---

[1] A socially approved institution involving the marriage of one man to two or more women at the same time. *Monogamy* is the marriage of one man to one woman while *polyandry* is the marriage of one woman to two or more men at the same time. *Polygamy* is a marriage of one individual to two or more spouses. This vague term which links *polygyny* and *polyandry* should be avoided whenever possible.

49

The Igbo acquire rights in women in many ways, but all must be validated by the payment of bridewealth. Until it was legally abolished in 1956, child marriage was the most common way of acquiring rights in women. The Igbo girl was betrothed early, sometimes before she was a year old. The prospective husband sent gifts to the girl and her mother, and sometimes helped the prospective father-in-law in farm work. The bridewealth payment might be deferred till the girl became of age. Some token of bridewealth might be accepted to encourage the prospective son-in-law.

Types of Marriage

Igbo marriage is an alliance between two families rather than a contract between two individuals. As far as the widow is concerned, death does not terminate the alliance. Widow inheritance is therefore a recognized and still prevalent institution. In this case a half siblingship is created for the children of the widow. Those children born "in the face of their father" inherit his property, whereas those born after the inheritance get their name and status from their mother's second husband. All these children still share the mother's hut.

"Woman marriage" is a recognized Igbo institution by which women can validate status in the society. Under this system, women "marry" in their own right by paying the bridewealth and have the right to dispose of their rights in their brides. Some women allow their husbands to exercise their rights and they accept their bride as a co-wife. If such female husbands have no children, their wives share the same hut with them and their children are adopted by the female husband. Generally female husbands found independent compounds and then let their brides choose *Iko* (lovers) who are acceptable to them to beget children by their "wives." Although there is a high correlation between economic power and female husbands, other categories of women who play this role include barren women, those who have lost all their children by death, and those who have only female children. There is no doubt that the institution of "woman marriage" benefits capable women by neutralizing the harsh effects of the Igbo inheritance law, which excludes women who have no male children from inheriting from their deceased husbands and excludes most women from inheriting from their agnatic lineages.[2]

There is a prescribed status-linked marriage between "yam-oriented" male and female children called *Njɔku* (*Ifɛjɔku*), and *Mmaji*, respectively. These children are usually born to members of the yam title society called ɛzɛ *ji* (yam chief). As the human representatives of the yam deity, these children are entitled to privileges. *Mmaji* must be the first wife of *Njɔku* as well as the only wife with *Mmaji* status. Other co-wives must not be *Mmaji*. *Njɔku* or *Mmaji* who is today a Christian must find a female or male opposite to marry. Though a Christian, he is forced by his culture, and often by fear, to

---

[2] Another term for a patrilineage, a social group (and in the Igbo case, a corporate social group) tracing descent from the male line only.

owe allegiance to two worlds—the traditional religion and the Christian faith.

"Wife exchange" is by no means a common Igbo marriage institution. The case which occurred at Nsirimo, my own village-group (about ten miles south of Umuahia) in 1952 shows the flexibility in the ways in which rights in women can be acquired in Igbo society. A, a man of about seventy who had four wives, fell in love with one of the three wives of B, a man from another village. B was then about fifty and his childless, unfaithful wife was about thirty-five. The love affair between A and B's wife reached a stage when they decided "to marry." The divorce came into effect when B's bridewealth payment was returned to him. B felt some humiliation over this, refused the bridewealth, and in retaliation set out to marry the only one of A's four wives he could possibly marry by the rule of exogamy. This woman of about forty had two sons. When the respective in-laws of A and B refused to involve themselves in this matter, and neither A nor B would accept the bridewealth payment made by the other, the two men simply exchanged their wives with some villagers acting as witnesses. Of the parties involved, only A has died since the exchange. Besides showing the flexibility of Igbo marriage customs, this case history points up another important fact: that married women form part of the marriageable population.

Acculturation has made possible the institutionalization of such other forms as church marriage, marriage by ordinance[3] and "Marriage by photograph." The latter developed during World War II under the "Send Me a Wife" program initiated by Igbo soldiers serving in Nigeria and overseas. Under this program, prospective grooms and brides who could not possibly meet for some time exchanged pictures and then made up their minds whether their respective families should proceed with the marriage negotiation. It is a system followed by some Igbo migrants who work in Fernando Póo and in Ghana and other west African countries.

Stages in the Marriage Process

No matter how the Igbo acquires a wife, the process of betrothing and marrying an Igbo girl is a long, ceremonious one. It often takes years and is seldom accomplished in months. Marriage is so important and central to the Igbo that nothing concerned with it is taken lightly. The whole process falls into four interrelated stages: asking the girl's consent, working through a middleman, testing the bride's character, and paying the bridewealth.

Who asks a girl's consent to marriage depends on the age of the prospective spouses and the circumstances under which the marriage will take place. In most arranged marriages the spouses are usually children and have no choice. Their parents and guardians select the spouses, whose consent is expected. In behalf of those who marry under the "Send Me a Wife" program, their friends and relatives do the asking. This contrasts with the Euro-American tradition, where

---

[3] A civil marriage contracted before a court registrar, who issues the couple a marriage license.

the emphasis on romantic love makes individual choice imperative. In Igbo society, it is the love growing out of the family created by the marriage that is emphasized.

The "consent to marriage" has been built into an elaborate ritual and is conducted through public channels. The middleman and other relatives of the prospective spouses exert their pressure. The diviner's opinion is sought as to the auspiciousness of the marriage. Other preliminary investigations center on the incidence of premature death, whether there are histories of twin births, whether the status is *osu* or *diala,* the divorce rate in the family, and whether the rules of exogamy are respected. If both families are satisfied with their inquiries, the courtship begins and ends with the payment of the bridewealth. In its institutional aspect, courtship involves all the members of the two families concerned. Presents are exchanged, relations become more friendly, and the qualities of the two families are critically observed. If nothing happens to break the courtship, the bridegroom's family makes a formal application by bringing a pot of raphia liquor or *nkwo ɛnu* (palm liquor), depending on the locality. This is repeated several times until "the asking money" is accepted by the bride's mother and father.

Then follows the stage know as *ɛagwa*—testing character. Under child marriage it may last many years; for adolescent girls, it is a matter of a few months. The girl is introduced to the prospective husband's home, during which time she is watched for social adjustment. Her capabilities in house crafts, her working habits, her temperament, her form and figure—all are observed. Every adult member of the extended family passes critical comments on the qualities and behavior of the new member. She is given the opportunity to make friends. After a month or two, she is decorated with *uri* (body painting) and sent back to her parents with rich presents, indicating that she has passed her test. Before this time, her mother had briefed her on the role of *"nwanyi ɔhuru"*—a girl under trial. During her subsequent visits to her prospective husband's home, the young bride is gradually introduced to all the family chores. She shares the household duties—cooking, marketing, and farming—according to her age and ability. Generally, the qualities desired in a bride are her manners; physical beauty is secondary. *"Agwa bɔ mma"*—"Good manners constitute beauty"—is an Igbo saying that has much meaning in this context. The new bride is expected to be respectful toward her elders, obedient to the older members of her new family, sociable with her playmates, clean and industrious in the home. Her virginity is taken for granted; indeed, it is insisted upon because the Igbo say that "a woman never forsakes a man who breaks her virginity."[4]

The settlement of the bridewealth is the next stage. It is a protracted business which requires sitting all night, no matter when it starts. The Igbo are good at haggling, and the place to demonstrate their art is at the marriage settlement. People discuss the good and the bad qualities of the bride. Members of the girl's lineage increase the bridewealth and the lineage of the husband diminishes it.

---

[4] However, acculturation has made this an ideal rather than a social fact. The long period of schooling, the increasing divorce rate, and the fact that the traditional "virginity" test is no longer insisted upon, or made public, indicate that the Igbo do not take a bride's virginity for granted nowadays.

But the customary bridewealth is known and precedents are not lacking. No haste is shown until all are thoroughly tired. Then the parties to the marriage sit down together to discuss the matter more seriously. When an agreement is finally reached, the husband's party rises and shakes hands with the wife's party "for demonstrating common sense at last." A reasonable proportion of the amount of bridewealth agreed upon is deposited. "Bridewealth is not fully paid," the Igbo say. "Full payment is made at death." "It does not end in a day," others say.

Once this installment is paid and accepted, custom permits sexual relations between the couple provided they are mature. Before this time, the bride is not a "wife." She is betrothed and her fiancé has no sexual access to her. It is the fiancé's mother's responsibility to preserve the chastity of the bride during the "trial stage."

Before the father takes the bridewealth, he gives his daughter a cup of palm liquor and asks her to show her husband to the audience by giving him the liquor. The shy girl walks with faltering steps to her husband, sips the liquor, and as she gives it to him, tells her shouting audience: "This is my husband. Father may take the bridewealth." As the money is counted and an agreement is made out (in fact, only the legal amount of £35 is recorded, the major part of the bridewealth payment being simply "witnessed") a lavish refreshment is served. The festivity which marks the rest of the evening is disturbed by the weeping which marks the separation of the bride from her lineage. The elderly women console the bride and her mother by reminding them that "what is involved is journey and not death."

The Adjustment of the New Bride

There is no doubt that the bride experiences problems of adjustment in her new home. This is especially true with very young ones, who tend to run to their natal home whenever they feel homesick, but they are not encouraged to stay and are usually sent back to their husband's home by their father. But for most girls, adjustment does not present many problems. They look forward with eagerness to the day when they will get married and they realize that marriage involves leaving their natal village.

A girl's life is essentially a preparation for marriage. Mothers lose no time in reminding their daughters that certain types of behavior cannot be tolerated from them. "You are not a boy but a girl. You must marry one day!" a comment frequently made by irritated mothers, seldom fails to put a deviant girl back to the Igbo way.

The role structure of an Igbo family is clear and is well understood by the new bride. A well-adjusted daughter makes a well-adjusted bride. In her natal home, the bride has seen how her father's or brother's new bride behaved. She remembers the advice her mother and other relatives gave her. She knows that her great objective in life is marriage; that a woman's glory is her children, and that to have children she must have a husband. This is a chance she cannot afford to miss. Although it is true that she has lost her friends in her own village, she can now make more permanent friends. In her new village are relatives already known to her and there may be many others. Women from her own village and from her mother's village and her father's mother's village may be married and living in her husband's village (an important function of exogamy). She sees them often and they make her welcome. Every market day she has the opportunity to see her mother and other relatives and to share gossip and news. As a new wife, she receives certain domestic privileges (for example, a favored share of meat), she is well clothed, she performs light tasks, she assumes more responsibilities, and, in time, she will soon have her own hut. If she is a good wife (that means living in peace with other wives and household members) and makes a success of her marriage, she will be in a position to play the role of middlewoman when girls from her own village are to be married into her husband's village.

Besides helping in the adjustment of the new bride, exogamy serves other social functions. It widens social links and gives a person a privileged position —okɛlɛ status—in his or her mother's natal village. The individual also acquires social links in his or her father's mother's natal village. The various villages where a man's married sisters—real or classificatory—live extend the bond of social relations. We may thus regard exogamy as fostering a horizontal linkage that has no vertical extension because of the nature of the political structure. Furthermore, the system of exogamy softens intervillage tension and extends the individual's economic sphere and security. This is indicated by the role of ɔmɔɔkpɔ—daughters married away—in ending intervillage and intravillage tension and disputes.

Igbo exogamy is not only based on biological principles. It also has a social foundation. It is the kinship principle in its social and biological sense that is generally applied. Strangers who live among Igbo communities are expected to conform to the principles of the village exogamy. This guarantees them the protection from violation they need for their daughters. Besides being a factor modifying the centrifugal forces of Igbo separatism, exogamy protects premarital ethics.

The "Big Compound" Ideal of the Igbo Family

The Igbo family is founded on a "big compound" ideal. A compound is considered "big" according to the number of people in it. A new bride is thus always a welcome member of this group.

A big compound depends on the ability of the compound head: it benefits from his influence. It is the demonstration of his personal achievement, his social status. There is therefore a correlation between socioeconomic status and the achievement of the "big compound" ideal. The social climber aims at this ideal; the successful man achieves it. He marries as many wives as he can maintain, that is, providing enough farm plots to help the women and their dependents make a living. Polgyny is conceived as imposing social and economic obligations which can be fulfilled only by a man of substantial means. It is a wealthy Igbo who marries many wives and is able to command the resources to keep them as well as attract agnates to his compound.

The Developmental Cycle of the "Big Compound"

A big compound is marked by a developmental cycle which is essentially segmentary in character. Within every generation the Igbo have sanctions which keep children in their father's compound. It is considered unfilial for a son to found an independent compound during the lifetime of his father. This makes a three-generational family possible but by no means common. With the death of one's father or one's compound head, (who may be father's brother or senior half brother), there is the tendency for the compound to move toward a new social alignment or a new social equilibrium because the internal dynamics of the existing compound have been upset. The property as well as the wives of the late compound head goes to his heirs. The inevitable conflicts between half brothers over property rights lead to fission, as is demonstrated when they found separate compounds or join the compounds of other agnates.

In its initial phase, a big compound may start with a domestic group as its nucleus, essentially a householding and housekeeping unit which provides part of the resources—material and sociocultural—needed for the enculturation[5] of its members. Its reproductive unit may be a nuclear family or a matrifocal unit[6] of a polygynous family. Other members of this domestic group are recruited through filiation, affinal links,[7] pawning, or apprenticeship. As the daughters marry they leave the domestic group and the sons' wives and the additional wives of the male householder join it, the bridewealth of the daughters paying that of the incoming wives. This is what the Igbo mean when they say that "wealth begat people and people begat people."

The second phase is marked by a pressure on the household farmland of the domestic group, a pressure resulting from increase in population. Some adult members of the compound who have become household heads in their own right demand more household farmland beyond the supply of the compound head. They leave to found compounds in a less congested area within the lineage land, but the adult sons of the compound head remain within the compound. Those who leave often attract with them the dissatisfied protégés of the compound head. With his death the whole cycle begins again. His children may join the

[5] A learning process (or a process of conditioning) by which an individual is made to acquire and assimilate the contents and values of his culture so that he can operate as an efficient member of his society.

[6] Sometimes called a matricentric family, it is a mother-centered segment of the polygynous family. Two or more *matrifocal units* "linked" to or sharing a husband (who may be male or female) result in a polygynous family. A matrifocal unit is structurally simpler than a *nuclear* family, which consists of a husband, wife, their children and other dependents. A matrifocal household consists of a mother, her children, and other dependents. Among the Igbo, it is essentially a cooking unit and an eating unit.

[7] Created by marriage and sometimes called relationships "in-law." Strictly speaking, I am an affine of my wife and all my wife's kinsmen save her affines. But as an Igbo, I include my wife's affines among my ɔgɔ-affines!

compounds of their father's brothers, found separate compounds, or unite under a responsible and diplomatic brother (sibling or half brother) who can accommodate the conflicting interests of all the members.

Today the new opportunities offered by the cities affect the big compound in two ways. There is a trend toward the stabilization of the "parent" compounds. The households of most migrants (whether full or split) and other professional men are attached to them. On the other hand, the fad for "country houses"—important modern status symbols—tends to disturb the old equilibrium. The location of the country houses depends on their accessibility to major roads rather than to household farmlands; moreover, they tend to have absentee compound heads and few able-bodied males.

New Trends in the Igbo Family System

Many other changes have taken place in the Igbo family system in the last fifty years. Christian marriage and marriage by ordinance are among the important innovations. Both have given women new legal protection and property rights not recognized by the traditional system, but they have also created new problems of adjustment for the couple. They have not, however, eliminated polygyny among people who had contracted marriages under the old system.

Although in 1956 the Eastern Nigerian Government legally limited the amount of bridewealth payment to £30 (£5 are added for "expenses"), and also abolished child marriage, the Igbo reaction shows that these customs have not greatly changed. Prospective husbands are not generally willing to take their prospective in-laws to court, nor are educated Igbo girls willing to force the hands of their parents through legal sanctions. As a result, bridewealth payment is still very high and, in some places, higher than the 1956 level. The amount demanded and paid reflects the educational level and the potential economic contribution of the prospective bride. Until the Igbo idea that education is a human investment which must yield returns to parents is changed, there will be no solution to this problem.

The present trend is toward an older marriage age for boys and girls, the result of a long period of schooling. Child marriage is slowly disappearing. Among the professional Igbo, the trend is toward a nuclear family, neolocal residence[8] (as long as they work away from home), and marriage based on love. Tension still builds around the amount of support that should be given to the members of the extended family. A few educated Igbo, especially the self-employed, traders, and government employees, see in polygyny a means of adjustment in their changing world. Their wives are rotated between their natal household and their place of work, thus giving an appearance of monogamous life. Some people still regard the village environment as the best one for the upbringing of youth, especially adolescent girls. This tends to create intergenerational conflict: the young people want to live in cities and their parents try to restrain them until they are "properly socialized" in the village.

---

[8] A newly married couple establishes a residence independent of, and sometimes away from, the parents of either.

6

Growing Up in an Igbo Village

MOTHERHOOD BRINGS AN important change in a woman's status, a change from a mistress who simply attracts and allures to a mother who shares the dignity of her husband and who has increased the lineage membership. Igbo women realize that the romantic aspect of the husband-wife relation does not last as long as the child-mother bond. Children are a great social insurance agency, a protection against dependence in old age. To have a male child is to strengthen both the social and the economic status, for it is the male child who inherits the father's property. A woman—and worse still, a man—who has no male child contemplates old age with particular horror.

Igbo Ideas about Conception

The biological facts of conception are accepted but other factors are also involved in pregnancy and are much more important: the consent of the deities and the willingness of dead lineage members and other friendly spirits to reincarnate themselves. The absence of either of these two agents renders conception impossible, the Igbo say.

Conception is treated as a normal phase of life. There is no generally recognized food taboo observed by the Igbo; what food is avoided reflects local bias and dietary habits. The general rule is that the pregnant woman should eat what she likes, the amount being regulated for a new mother by her mother-in-law.

The navel is extremely important, and concern about it begins before birth. A pointed navel is desired. A woman becomes fond of a child whose navel she admires and gives this child occasional presents. *Aŋara*—a common type of garden fruit—is ritually touched to such a child's navel; the pregnant woman eats a part of this fruit and gives a part to the child to eat. The idea is to make her own unborn baby acquire the shape of the navel she admires. After her delivery, she is asked not to touch certain things; otherwise the navel may not have the desired form.

Certain births are *nsɔ*, (*alθ*)—taboo—among the Igbo. The birth of twins was regarded as a great calamity. The mother was isolated and the children were destroyed. The navel cords were not severed. It was believed that human beings should propagate their species by single births. For a woman to bear more than one child at a time was regarded as degrading humanity to the level of beasts. "Plural offspring is nature's law for goats, cats, and dogs, not for men," the people say. Other births regarded as abnormal but less seriously punished were children born feet first, and those born with teeth.

A Child Is Born

The place of delivery may be in the husband's compound or in the woman's father's compound. The actual delivery takes place in a woman's backyard, which is usually either fenced or walled around. Except in complicated cases, male assistants are not employed. In some cases, it is the crying babe who alerts the members of the compound. Some women have told me that they never needed any help, adding that such was also true of their mothers.

For women who need help—and most of them do—a tree in the backyard or a pole specially planted is grasped during delivery to facilitate "pushing down" the baby. When labor is prolonged the compound head is asked to pour a libation of water to the ancestors. The woman is asked to examine her conscience as to the possibility that the sex taboo on "day coitus" was infringed. (It is believed that coitus in the daytime delays the placenta.) The duty of the local midwife is to determine the right time to bear down. When this is decided, the women around bear down in sympathy. Children are expected to cry vigorously at birth in order to be welcome. The cries of the baby are greeted with thunderous applause by the woman attendants. Obscene demonstrations characterize the scene. Women look for the husband to give him a beating on the hips—a symbol of fruitful sexual activity.

The Umbilical Cord

The severing of the umbilical cord is a dramatic event. A small native blade, triangular in shape and sharpened at the base, is used. With this blade—*aguwa*—in her right hand, the midwife, pretending to cut very close to the base of the cord, asks:

"Do you want me to cut here?"

"No! No! No!" is the shouted reply. The midwife continues to ask this question and receives the same answer until she touches the right place, about six to eight inches from the base of the umbilical cord, which is then cut. The placenta is buried at the site of the birth and the baby is bathed. The mother and the baby are taken into a hut, where a fire has been made for them. She shares the same bed, often little more than a heap of earth, with her babe. To put a baby in a separate place is regarded as showing want of love for the baby and little respect for one's duty as a mother. However, educated Igbo women have rejected this idea, which is still firmly entrenched among their less educated sisters.

Babies are very expensive. It is, however, considered a joy to spend for them. The husband is obliged to show his love for his wife as well as his social status by displaying what Veblen called conspicuous consumption. Everybody is welcome to see the baby; indeed, not to visit a mother and her baby is a most serious offense. There is entertainment for all. To come as often as one has the opportunity is a mark of good neighborliness. Not only must people be entertained; they expect to see what is put up for the mother. Among the southern Igbo, the leaves of a split palm frond are used as hangers for stockfish (dried cod and haddock imported from Norway and Sweden), snails, the skull of a goat slaughtered for the mother, and other food. To protect the husband from the unkind criticisms of late visitors, consumed foods must show their traces by means of empty fish racks, tails of stockfish, snail shells, skulls of goats, and so on. A mother who leaves the seclusion without "adding flesh" to her body is gossiped about by other women: "She is not kindhearted," they will say, or "She ate like a hippopotamus and still showed a skeleton."

While the mother and her babe are in their seclusion, the child's umbilical cord is tended with care until it falls off. The fall is hastened by the application of an oily matter into which ɵda—a local herb—is added. When it falls off, in about four days, its burial is delayed until the child is named.

Circumcision takes place about eight days after the birth of a male infant. The mother leaves the compound for the first time on this day. She is escorted to the household farm, where she collects a few things for the ritual. The circumcision is performed by a skilled woman in the village. In southern Igbo communities, a girl waits until maturity before her clitoridectomy[1] which takes place during her *Mgbɛdɛ*. This fattening seclusion was quite common, though not always followed by clitoridectomy, in many other Igbo communities.

The burial of the umbilical cord is not marked by an elaborate ritual but its social significance is great. It has given rise to a social institution which may be called "the navel complex." The Igbo who cannot point to the burial place of his navel cord is not a *diala*—freeborn. A child whose navel cord was not buried is denied citizenship. For its burial, the mother selects the most fruitful oil palm tree out of the many that the husband may indicate. At the foot of this tree the umbilical cord is buried. In time, the child is led to build around his "tree of status" such sentiments and emotional attachment which are embedded in the phrase *nkwɵ alɵm* ("The palm for my navel cord"). This palm belongs to the child. It cannot be alienated. Not only is it a symbol of *diala* status; it is the foundation for the socially ambitious.

---

[1] Female circumcision involving the excision of the clitoris; among some Igbo communities, it is preceded by a "fattening" seclusion (*Mgbɛdɛ*) of an adolescent girl.

A Child Is Named

Receiving a name is an important event in a child's life for he is socially accepted as soon as he is given a name. The "name-giving" ceremony, a formal occasion celebrated by feasting and drinking, is also an occasion which generally articulates the different social groups to which the child belongs.

"Names are not merely considered as tags by means of which individuals may be distinguished, but are intimately associated with various events in the life of the individual as well as those of the family and the larger social group" (Wieschhoff 1941:212). A child is given many names. The parents' choice of names may be dictated by the character of its birthmarks and by the diviner's opinion. *Njɔku* and *Mmaji,* the male and female figures of the yam deity, are conferred by divination. Other names may be given to show the market day on which a child was born, or the preference for boys, or a certain concern for the future of the child. *Nwanyimɛolɛ*—"What can a woman do?"—shows that a father is in need of a male child. *Ɔnwubiko*—"May death forgive"—shows that parents have lost many of their children by death and pray that this child may thrive. *Chukwuɛmɛka*—"God has done well"—is a thanksgiving name for the favor received. *Nwaokoriɛ*—male child born on *oriɛ* market day—shows the day of the birth of the child.

The next important phase in the life of the child is teething. The period is watched with great anxiety. It may mark a turning point in a child's life if he cuts the upper teeth before the lower ones. The first person who notices a child's new tooth gives him a hen. This is not an outright present. The increase of this hen is shared equally between the two. The gift of the hen establishes a firm friendship tie between the child and his benefactor, a friendship which extends to other members of the family.

"Churching"—An Outing Ceremony

An "outing ceremony" for the mother and child is another important social event. The traditional place was the village market. Today, *ifɵ ahia*—"exhibition at the marketplace"—has been replaced by what is called "churching." In its reinterpreted form, the traditional elements of "showing wealth"—feasting, and drumming—have been retained, but a religious rite has been added to what was a purely secular affair. The guests make presents of money and receive pieces of meat whose market value is about a third of that of their presents. However, the guest's gift is expected to be returned doubled and so the feasting is proportionately increased. Great indebtedness has sometimes resulted from these ceremonies and the foundations of friendships have been threatened by a person's inability to honor these obligations. It must be pointed out that this reciprocity is not restricted to "churching" but is extended to all forms of ceremonies in which a formal feast is held. There is no legal sanction against one who fails to return a gift but the social sanction is great: the loss of status and the pressure from wives who have been beneficiaries of such gifts may force a man to borrow to meet obligations of this sort.

The Igbo are very fond of children. Their infants and toddlers are petted and overindulged, especially the *nwa-olu*—only child—and the *ɔdɵ nwa* —the tail child, as the last-born child is called. Such a child is the darling of everybody and is suckled the longest. As is well known the world over, such wide latitude tends to spoil them. Even the *ɔdɵ nwa* admit this and blame some of their lack of skills on the indulgence of their parents. "I didn't go to school because my parents just would not let me," one last-born child said regretfully.

But for most children this period of indulgence and attention is short-lived, and the transition to a role of responsibility may be a traumatic experience. The lavish affection accorded infants ends with the arrival of the next baby. The older child is no longer suckled and feels rejected. It is to the father's mother and the mother's mother that he then turns for affection. He is expected to become a responsible older child without having been taught how to be one. In time, he comes to realize that he must accept this new status and he learns to cooperate. He keeps watch over his younger sibling when his mother is away. The dog is his faithful companion. Other children join him for a while and then go out to play. If he can carry the baby straddled over his back, he joins their company; otherwise he stays with his faithful friend, the dog. When the baby cries he gives it water. The dog is more than a companion: it provides the only dependable "diaper service" by licking up the baby's excretions; and it also creates some drama in attempting to keep other dogs away—a drama that frightens both infant and brother.

The Igbo Child Shares Two Worlds

Unlike American children, who are often confined to their own world, Igbo children grow up and participate in two worlds—the world of children and the world of adults. Igbo children take an active part in their parents' social and economic activities. They are literally everywhere. They are taken to the market, to the family or village tribunal, to funerals, to a feast, to the farm, and to religious ceremonies. They help entertain their parents' guests. There are no children's parties which they are encouraged to dominate, nor are there parents' parties from which they are excluded. If there is a social or ritual ceremony going on in an Igbo village, everybody is welcome. Igbo children do not have private sleeping rooms. In their early years they sleep in their mother's hut; later, when the boys are in their late teens, they sleep in their own huts. Girls sleep with their mothers until they leave the family after marriage.

Igbo children participate in the affairs of the adult world with childlike enthusiasm; in their own world they dramatize adult roles and spend their leisure hours doing "nursery" cooking, playing father and mother, holding "play" markets and mock fights.

Life in the family group is informal. In the usual eating arrangement the girls eat with their mother and the boys with their father. When a guest is present, all the children eat with the mother and the guest eats with the father. Otherwise the members of a domestic group may eat from the same pot. For an unusual reason as well as because of the general scarcity of animal meat, children get little protein. The Igbo elders believe that a generous allowance of meat to a child may make him steal and be wasteful in later life. Although the upbringing of children is the responsibility of all the members of the compound, each mother has the primary duty of feeding her children and the members of her own hut.

Children are brought up in the open. The village center as well as the centers of each lineage segment, called *mbara ama,* is a hub of social activity. It is the place where most children receive much of their informal education, meet with their age-mates, try their strength in wrestling and in the inevitable intralineage contests and mock fights. Such activities make social life competitive. At each *mbara ama* children are found playing in the sand a common game called *nsa.* This game requires a ring about two inches in diameter which is made of string. The leader buries it in a heap of sand and other players dip their sticks into the sand in order to center the ring. The first player to center the ring wins a right to play. The player whose ring is not centered by any of the contestants wins a point. The last player to win a right to play either is hit by all the rest with their sticks or his outstretched palm, resting on a hill of sand, is beaten by each winner.

The *mbara ama* is a place that affords recreation and entertainment for all. A bevy of girls may be seen dancing with great enjoyment, their waists heavily ringed with colored beads, a costly expenditure for a newly married man. (A wife denies her husband the consummation of their marriage until he buys expensive beads for her. This is also a compensation paid to her for preserving her virginity.)

Some boys may engage in archery contests. At one end of the *mbara ama* may be found older boys deeply involved in a game of *okwε,*[2] while elderly men are engaged in the more serious work of preparing the cordage for the farming season. Adults lounge around in a leisurely manner when the day's work is over.

Children take an active and important part in the work of the compound and the village. Matmaking and carrying mud for house building are services which children are expected to render to any villager. Food is the only reward for such communal work. Children fetch firewood and carry water in large gourds or in clay pots skillfully balanced on their heads. A child who breaks a pot is expected to cry to express his sorrow; otherwise he gets a whipping. By engaging in

---

[2] A game of beads which requires one board with two rows, each having at least five pits (called "houses"). The minimum number of players is two. The ten houses (sometimes more) contain ten beads each. Each player "owns" the five houses facing him. He plays by distributing all the contents of one house (except one bead) consecutively in an anticlockwise direction, dropping only one bead at a time into each house. Which house a player distributes depends on his strategy for winning the game. In one form of this game, all houses starting with the terminal house (the one in which the last bead was dropped), containing odd numbers below ten (1, 3, 5, 7, 9) may be won (or in Igbo idiom, "eaten").

these activities, children get to know their age-mates informally and thus develop friendships with them.

In adolescence the age-grade system assumes a formal character. Schooling has affected this institution. In the preschool days, adolescent boys passed through a formal initiation known as *ima ɔgwɵ*—a rite of passage which enabled them to acquire aggressive medicine. Girls passed through *mgbɛdɛ,* a ceremonial seclusion known as the "fat house." Today it is the social division of labor and the needs of village life that have preserved the informal age-set institution. The age grades represent their villages in intervillage dances and wrestling competitions. They contribute financially to the welfare programs of the village-group, censor the morality of their members, heighten their funeral ceremonies, and provide the essential pressure groups which make for change in political and social life.

Wrestling is a popular Igbo sport shared by all. The Igbo are extremely boastful of their skill in wrestling, present or past. The most thrilling bouts are intervillage-group wrestling competitions where the characteristic tricks and twists of each group are demonstrated. Wrestling is done to the accompaniment of music. Maneuvering includes crouching, pulling out of tight corners, dodging, twisting, and turning at great speed. When opponents come to grips strength and endurance are tested. With arms interlocked, legs rigid, heads pushing hard, they pull, twist, strain, and pant. The excited spectators shout encouraging words to their favorites and often twist their own limbs in empathy. Evenly matched opponents are separated as "draws." Wrestlers must not scratch or bite each other. To fall on one's buttocks or one's back means defeat; it is a victory to lift the opponent up by a few inches from the ground. Wrestling leads to lifelong friendships between equally matched partners. Many bouts may lead to fighting, but by allowing competitors a fair chance elders ensure that the peace is not disturbed.

Learning the Igbo way involves constant adjustment to competitive situations. The domestic group, the play group, the age grade, and the wider Igbo society are extremely competitive, each with its own rules. But all share one characteristic: an emphasis on open competition and a differential reward for the winner and the loser.

$$\boxed{7}$$

The Kinship Network

ORMALLY THE IGBO CHILD is brought up in his father's lineage. Later in his childhood, he is constantly brought into contact with his mother's lineage. As he grows up he is made increasingly aware of the wider social world, the most important of which are his father's mother's lineage and his mother's mother's lineage. When he marries he acquires affinal links, his wife's lineage playing an important role in the social life of his children. These five lineages, each of which is a distinct agnatic group, constitute for the Igbo their most important kinship network. The quality of interpersonal relations which exist in or among these five agnatic groups differs; their respective interests are often conflicting, but from the point of view of the individual Igbo this conflict is in his own best interest. It helps him to maneuver among these agnatic groups, playing one group against the other in the interest of self-protection and social advancement.

The Agnates

Igbo is a society with a strong patrilineal emphasis. The whole society can be mapped into a number of agnatic groups. Since agnation determines the membership of a family group, the line of inheritance and succession to name and office, a person takes most of his jural rights in land and in social, economic, and political positions from the lineage of his father. The members of this lineage are his ɵmɵnna (agnates).

As the Igbo say: ɵmɵnna bɵ ikɛ ("The agnates are the source of one's strength"). Rights over the use of land depend primarily on agnatic descent, and secondarily on local residence. A person depends on his agnates "to get up"; they provide social security and comfort. They support his just claims against other groups. They provide the ladder needed in social climbing. It is to one's lineage that a person brings his wife after marriage; it is among his lineage members that he rears his children and gives them their stake in life.

Title-taking ceremonies, marriage feasts, second-burial rites, and other ceremonies through which a wider social group is activated succeed or fail because of the type of interpersonal relations between a person and his agnates.

It is the prayer of the Igbo to die among their agnates and be buried in their ancestral land. Normally the corpse of a married woman who died in her husband's home is brought back to be buried among her kinsmen. But if a woman had achieved a high social status and had expressed the desire to be buried in her husband's home, a "death duty" is usually paid to her agnates. It is then the duty of her sons to make a cement tomb (a symbol of high social status) for her. It is the duty of the agnates who live "abroad" (a duty now performed by the Family Improvement Unions) to bring a dead agnate home for burial. Where this cannot possibly be done, the deceased agnates perform ǫpǫhgǫ— a rite that will return the soul of the deceased to his ancestral land.

The ideal behavior expected among agnates may be characterized as "brotherliness"—that is, brotherliness as defined by mutual trust, help, loyalty, and affection. A person may achieve security through loyalty to and cooperation with his agnates. The extension of respect-relationships is another mode of adjustment among agnates. A person recognizes and appreciates the high social status achieved by his agnates, boasts of them, and may place himself under them so as to advance socially in turn.

Great concern is expressed for the future. Successful agnates are consulted for advice, and in many cases even before a person asks for advice, it is thrust on him: "Do you not see the progress others are making? Are you not of our blood?" This is sufficient to set a delinquent Igbo thinking. Today, education is regarded as the most important source of security. To deny a brilliant child a good education is to deny the coming generation a better place in life. Although the Igbo expresses great anxiety for the future and may feel much frustration in connection with personal failures or lack of self-advancement, he regards self-pity as unmanly. Rather, he resorts to self-criticism to assert the man he is. "Is it because I have not taken the 'yam title' that you ride on me?" he thunders to an opponent, who is now completely disarmed.

If the agnates are the greatest prop of success, they are also the greatest source of hostility. The same Igbo who tell us that the agnates are the source of strength also confess that the agnates also kill. It is the house rat, not the bush rat, that knows where the mother keeps her condiments. It is the agnates who accuse, attribute, and convict a person of sorcery. It is always the agnate who is convicted of sorcery. Withdrawal, personal detachment, and fear of intimacy are traits attributed to sorcerers. It is the agnate who is required to be near, be personally involved, and be intimate with other agnates. Sorcery attribution—nshi— (not witchcraft) is the most feared form of direct aggression and is directed at secretive persons who do not speak their mind, who have "something to hide."

Direct aggression is seen in child beating, wife beating, challenging an adversary to a wrestling contest instead of carrying complaints to the compound head, boasting, quarreling, and fighting. Women manifest much aggression of the indirect, verbal sort. The sharpest weapon of indirect aggression, the tongue, is the favorite of women. Women gossip about everything and anything. Someone's indiscreet love affair, a lazy man or woman, the schoolboy who could not pass his examinations, "the son from the white man's country" who does not help the village, "the son abroad" who returned home with no wealth, and, of course, co-wives are some of their targets. Social inferiors express their hostility indirectly through secret destruction of property, deprecation, envy, and obstinacy.

The Mother's Agnates

Relationship with one's *umunɛ*—one's mother's lineage—presents a striking contrast to the relationship with one's patrilineage. A person is a privileged honorary member in his mother's lineage. It is a place where he is made most welcome. He does not normally inherit property or office from this lineage; rather he depends on his mother's agnates to protect his jural rights in his patrilineage. He seeks their support in any serious case in which he is involved. If convicted of sorcery, his *umunɛ* is the only place for his exile. When conditions become unbearable in his lineage, he seeks voluntary exile there. The title taker, the student who plans to go to the "white man's country" for higher education, and the *mgbɛdɛ girls*—debutantes—who are coming out of the "fattening house" preparatory to marriage, depend on their *umunɛ* for substantial contributions and gifts. They are the social events which activate important kinship groups.

The *umunɛ* kinship bond is a permanent one, unaffected by the marital status of the mother and unchanged when she dies. Rather, the death of one's mother strengthens one's relationship with her lineage. The dead woman is expected to receive a burial befitting her social status. To give one's mother and father expensive burials is regarded as one of the great tests of manhood. The Igbo say that a child who has not buried his parents properly cannot boast of having conquered life's problems. The death of a mother may create one of those rare occasions when the relationship between a person and his *umunɛ* is strained. The mother's agnates must satisfy themselves that their "daughter" was not neglected, and that she was well attended by her children. Sanctions against maltreating a mother vary from the imposition of fines to the refusal to authorize burial. Though often threatened in order to exact heavier fines, the latter is seldom invoked. According to Igbo law, the right to the corpse or the right to authorize burial belongs to the deceased's lineage. When this right was flouted in a northern Ngwa village, the injured party—in this case the dead woman's lineage—reported to the police department that their "daughter" had been beaten to death by her husband. The investigating policemen insisted on having the corpse dug up and removed to the nearest hospital for *post mortem* examination. The panic and inconvenience this caused the villagers taught a lesson which has not been forgotten.

Although he has no authority, the mother's brother, one of the most important persons in the life of the sister's son, exerts a great influence over him. When advice from friends and relatives fail to persuade the sister's son to a desired point of view, similar efforts of the mother's brother succeed. His influence stems from friendship and love rather than from fear and superiority. The special relation between the mother's brother and the sister's son is phrased by the Igbo in the idiom of the navel cord. They say that "both of them are held by the same navel cord"—in other words, a great maternal bond.

The sister's son enjoys a special status in the lineage of the mother's brother. He may not spill his blood while he is there; he may not be so provoked that he decides to bounce his buttocks on the ground, nor may he stamp a pestle on the ground. For him to do any of these is taboo, an offense to the earth-goddess. It is his *umunɛ* who must bear the consequences of his action. While he stays with his mother's brother, he is treated with much affection and allowed a wide latitude in his behavior. His playmates are warned against the danger of making him spill his blood. He jokes at the expense of everybody, his mother's father, his mother's brother and their wives. This joking relationship is extended to all the members of the mother's brother's lineage. It is the privilege of the sister's son to take anything from his mother's brother's house without asking for permission. The fruit trees in the latter's village are at his disposal without his asking permission. When he cannot buy enough palm wine[1] to entertain his guests, he goes to his mother's brother's lineage to "poach" liquor—an expedition which earns congratulations for the most adroit poachers.

The "Remote" Kinsmen

The father's mother's and the mother's mother's lineages constitute a person's "remote" kinsmen. They are nevertheless important in the life of a successful Igbo. The relations with one's mother's mother's agnates are more solid than those with one's father's mother's agnates. In none of these social groups, however, does the Igbo command any generally defined privileges. They assure him of support, and their members attend his feasts and title-taking ceremonies but they grant "poaching" privileges only to his father and his mother's brother. An Igbo who is the sister's son's son in one group or the sister's daughter's son in another group is forbidden to marry a girl directly descended from any members of these groups.

Balancing Kinship Conflicts

It must have become apparent from this discussion that a person resolves major conflicts in his ɵmɵnna by appealing for support, in the first instance, from his mother's agnates. His "second line of defense" comes from his father's mother's agnates and his mother's mother's agnates. The relation between the father and his son's mother's agnates is one of potential hostility; he owes them final bridewealth payment, which is a source of friction. By appealing to them for support against his father, the son is, in effect, resolving

---

[1] Another name for raphia liquor and palm liquor.

conflict through the extension of conflict. But the father's relation with his own mother's agnates (the father's *umune*) is very friendly. They are the people who can most easily disarm him through persuasion. A son finds that it is in his own interest to appeal to all loyalties in conflicting situations. Conflict resolution between a son and a father is therefore achieved through the manipulation of these delicately balanced agnatic groups.

Naming the Kin

The terms the Igbo employ for classifying these agnatic groups and for naming the members of each vary. Although "this situation may be confusing to the investigator, it is not necessarily so to the Ibo. Every Ibo is conversant with kinship terms within and often far beyond the radius in which he may seek a wife, just as he is aware of dialectical variations in any other field of terminology" (Ardener 1954: 85). The description of Igbo kinship terminology that follows uses the agnatic model through which the social groups are approached.

It has been stressed that every Igbo belongs to an agnatic group, a lineage with an unbroken continuity of descent in the male line. This agnatic group (patrilineage), as well as all its members, or agnates, is called by the same term, *ɵmɵnna. Ɵmɵnna* is, in one frame of reference, an exogamous unit. All its female members who must leave the lineage at marriage are called *ɵmɵ-ɔkpɵ*. In another frame of reference it is a term for agnates, meaning "children of father," its singular being *nwanna*. It does not distinguish between sex or generation but can be made to do so by the addition of more descriptive phrases.

By the rule of exogamy and virilocal residence,[2] we expect to meet non-agnates as *resident* members of a lineage; ego's mother is one. Ego's father is *nna,* and his mother is *nnɛ*. All his father's brothers and his father's sisters senior to ego are given classificatory terms: *dɛdɛ* (deɛ), *nna ukwu* and *daa* (dada), respectively, terms which distinguish between generation and sex but can be applied to ego's senior full siblings and senior half siblings. Ego's father's father is called *nnanna* and his father's mother, *nnɛnnɛ*, the latter literally means "mother's mother"—a term which is also applied to ego's actual mother's mother. Ego's father's wives other than his mother are called *nwunyɛ nna* (*nwunyɛ dɛdɛ*).

In a polygynous household, a distinction is made between ego's full siblings (children of the same mother), who are called *ɵmɵnnɛ* (*nwannɛ,* singular) and ego's half siblings (children by other wives of ego's father), who are called *ɵmɵnna* (*nwanna,* singular), irrespective of *age or sex. Ɵmɵnnɛ* constitute "one eating unit" and are symbolically referred to as children from one, *ɔnu usokwu*—"kitchen door"—but *ɵmɵnna,* even in its simplest frame of reference, does not.

---

[2] Virilocal residence results when a couple establishes a household with the husband's parents.

Ego calls his wives *nwanyi* and they call him *di*—"husband." Ego's children are ɘmɘ, a classificatory term extended to the children of his sons, the children of his son's sons, and all those who are of the same age as ego's children. Each individual child is termed *nwa*. Ego makes an important status distinction among ɔ*para*—his eldest son; *ada*—his eldest daughter; and ɔ*dɘ nwa*—his last child; the latter term is applied to the last child of each of ego's wives. More will be said about their roles in Chapter 10. A further distinction is made in terminology between ɔ*para* and *ada* on the one hand and ego's ɔ*para nnɛ*—mother's eldest son (who may be ego)—and *ada nnɛ*—ego's mother's eldest daughter. Although ego's sons' children of any sex are collectively termed *nwanwa*, ego's daughter's children (who are not members of his lineage) are termed *okɛlɛ* (*okɛnɛ*). *Okɛlɛ* status, as was noted earlier, confers honorary membership and guarantees privileges and license in ego's mother's lineage (*umunɛ*).

The Igbo use the term *umunɛ* in two senses: as a place name for ego's mother's natal village, and to refer to all ego's mother's agnates. *Anam aga ɛbɛ umunɛ m*—"I am going to my mother's natal village"—illustrates the former; ɔ*bɘ onyɛ umunɛ m*—"He [or she] belongs to my mother's natal village"—illustrates the latter. Ego's mother's father is *nna ocɛ* (ancient father) while his mother's mother is either *nnɛ nnɛ*, a descriptive term, or *nnɛ ocɛ* (ancient mother). Ego is termed *okɛlɛ*, (*okɛnɛ*) by all ego's mother's agnates. Ego extends to his mother's brothers and sisters senior or junior to him the appropriate terms which he applies to members of his own ɘmɘnna *and* ɘmɘnnɛ groups. For instance, his mother's brothers—full or half-siblings—senior to ego are termed *dɛdɛ* (*dɛɛ*), while those junior to him are termed ɘmɘnnɛ (*nwannɛ*, singular). One important departure in terminology must be noted. The term *nwannɛ* used by ego for his mother's brother's children and other relatives is not reciprocal as it is in ego's lineage. But *nwannɛ* is a reciprocal term between his mother's sister's children who share the same *umunɛ*, the same *nnɛ nnɛ* (*nnɛ ocɛ*), and *nna ocɛ*.

Ego's father's mother's natal village and ego's mother's mother's natal village are his *umunɛ ukwu*—great *umunɛ*. It is therefore axiomatic that ego's father's *umunɛ* and his mother's *umunɛ* (which are different local units by the rules of exogamy) become ego's great *umunɛ*. Ego applies the same term, *nna ocɛ ukwu*—great *nna ocɛ*—to his mother's mother's father, and another term, *nnɛ ocɛ ukwu*—great *nnɛ ocɛ*—to his mother's mother's mother and father's mother's mother. "Although these relatives themselves may be dead, their male descendants are known collectively to ego as his *umunɛ ukwu*, to members of which he is known as *okɛlɛ ukwu*" (*okɛnɛ* ukwu) (Ardener 1954:94).

The in-law relationship creates a wide range of affinal links which are termed ɔ*gɔ*—a reciprocal term which subsumes all generations and both sexes. The *umunɛ* members of ego's half siblings (who are ego's father's wives' villagers) are also termed ɔ*gɔ;* so also are ego's sons and son's sons *umunɛ* members. Although ego's in-laws are simply termed ɔ*gɔ*, he distinguishes between his father's in-laws—ɔgɔ nna—and his son's in-laws—ɔgɔ nwam. Although the father-in-law—ɔgɔ nwoko (male-in-law)—is distinguished from the mother-in-law— ɔgɔ nwanyi (female in-law)—these terms are applied to any male or female member (whether agnates or merely residents) of the father-in-law's village.

This description of Igbo kinship terminology shows how flexible the system is. It is a classificatory type in which many terms are extended to cover the widest possible range of kinship. There is more emphasis on seniority than on generation and the terminology shows the importance attached to siblingship. In ego's generation, older brothers and older sisters are generally distinguished, the distinction between full siblings and half siblings becomes clearly marked, whereas in another frame of reference younger siblings are lumped together. Grandparents are distinguished by sex, and terms for them are extended to their siblings. Another important feature of this kinship system is the strong, durable ties with the mother's and mother's mother's agnates, which contrast with the relatively weaker ties with the father's mother's agnates and the father's father's mother's agnates.

Terms of address are governed by rules which guide and regulate social interaction. Among many other features, Igbo kinship terminology embodies the *principle of respect* relationship. This requires a junior person to call his seniors *dɛdɛ* (*dɛɛ*)—"a term of respect" based on seniority and always addressed to a senior by a junior and never used among age equals. Reinforcing the "principle of respect" terminology is what might be called the principle of "superiority of praise name." Briefly stated, this principle recognizes the superiority of one's praise name or status name over all other appropriate kinship terms of address. A titled man's praise name tends to take precedence over all other terms of address. *Akunwannɛ* ("Mother's Wealth"), *Igwɛ* ("Heavens"), and *Ogbuɛhi* ("Cow Killer"), for example, are praise names which replace other forms of address.

8

Igbo Hospitality

THE IGBO are nothing if not hospitable. To them hospitality is a major social obligation. Inability to meet it is a humiliating experience for the Igbo. The general complaint of farmers after the planting season concerns the scarcity of yams with which to feed their guests. Their own need for yams, even when most pressing, is seldom discussed, although women may be far from silent about it. But unwillingness to meet the demands of hospitality is another matter: it leads to loss of prestige. The inhospitable person is called many names (none complimentary)—*onyε ani, onyε akpi, onyε aka chichi*—"the tight-fisted one." In Igbo estimation he is an unsocialized "person with a dry heart."

Igbo hospitality is a simple and spontaneous affair. It may be expressed in various ways: exchanging gifts and farm products, sharing meals, providing lodging and food for guests, and formally presenting kola nuts. And because hospitality is so simple in its expression, it is expected from everybody—rich and poor. "There is no individual at the head of the village whose obligation it is to entertain strangers or to provide food for the villagers in times of shortage. This attribute of chieftainship which is found in some parts of Africa is here lacking as is its converse, the right to levy tribute" (Green 1947: 36).

Principles of Hospitality

Hospitality is based on two principles: *direct* reciprocity and *indirect* reciprocity. Neighbors not only expect but demand that hospitality be directly reciprocal. As one Igbo song phrases it: "The drinker of other people's liquor, when shall we drink your own liquor?" With guests and visitors who meet for the first time at the home of an Igbo host, as well as itinerant traders and medicine men who carry on their professions in various villages, hospitality is based on the principle of *indirect* reciprocity. The guest who receives free lodging and food

71

is expected to return the same hospitality to any other traveler. "We are all travelers," the Igbo say, "and no traveler ever forgets his experiences." It is the Igbo's genuine desire to please his guests, even if doing so costs him the household meal or involves some form of indebtedness: "When my guest departs peacefully and satisfied, let my creditors come."

For the Igbo hospitality is not a form of charity, not a matter of doles from the rich to the poor. It is an expression of good neighborliness, the Igbo way of sociability. Hospitality symbolizes that a guest is welcome, though there have been cases in real life as well as themes in Igbo folk tales in which wicked people have concealed wicked designs behind a façade of hospitality. The story of the tortoise and the leopard illustrates this:

> The tortoise, a small, unobtrusive, and inoffensive animal, is the Igbo trickster, their symbol of patience, wisdom, sagacity, and cunning. One day, at the height of a famine season, when all the animals were starving, the tortoise encountered a leopard that had been preying on other animals, a fact well known to the tortoise. As the tortoise was passing the leopard's gate, he was invited to come in for kola nut. When the tortoise refused this hospitality, the following dialogue with the leopard began:
> "Come in for kola nut, my dear friend," requested the leopard.
> "No thank you. Nobody eats my kola nuts at home," replied tortoise.
> "Come in for a drink," insisted the leopard.
> "My liquor at home is growing sour for want of guests," said the tortoise.
> "Come and take my daughter to marriage," the leopard urged.
> "My daughter at home wants a husband," replied the tortoise.
> "Come and take a cow," the leopard pleaded.
> "Which should take the other—the cow or the tortoise?"
> "Which is your way—the grove path or the 'clean' path?" asked the leopard, now thoroughly exasperated.
> "The 'clean' path is my way; the grove path is bushy," replied the tortoise most deceitfully.

As the tortoise anticipated, the leopard hunted for him along the "clean" path while he moved safely through the grove path. The moral of this little tale is that the recipient of hospitality should have his wits about him.

Forms of Hospitality

The Igbo expect occasional conflicts in their interpersonal relations. Such conflicts notwithstanding, it is the Igbo ideal that good relations among neighbors be maintained. Evidence of good neighborliness is shown in the exchange of greetings, which the Igbo love to exchange. Westerners who have been to Igboland are often impressed (a few are, in fact, bothered) by the shouts of "*Onyɛ ɔca, nnɔ*!!" ("White fellow, welcome! welcome!"), which seem to be endless. Convention demands that inferiors show their respect for superiors by greeting them whenever both meet. Refusal to exchange greetings indicates a strained relationship; among women, it may degenerate into "fighting" with eyes, into quarrels, and even into real fighting. Strangers who cannot find their way or who need help of some kind have no difficulty among the Igbo—provided they remember that among this people greeting comes before anything else. Strangers who do not remember to greet their Igbo hosts may be accorded no hospitality. In the Igbo view, such strangers are fools: they have not been properly brought up.

Eating and drinking together are other forms of hospitality expected among neighbors and extended to visitors. Visitors and neighbors are expected and are formally invited to share meals with their hosts. For the Igbo, this is not just mere courtesy; it is sincere. To refuse this hospitality is considered a grave insult. The host may feel that he has been snubbed or is suspected of sorcery. His wife leaves the guest or the neighbor in no doubt of her feelings: "Is it because I cannot cook as delicious a meal as your wife or mother does?" is a typical remark. Even though a visitor has already eaten elsewhere, convention dictates—and good manners demand—that he at least taste his host's meal; only then can he plead "a full stomach" as a valid excuse from sharing the remainder of the repast.

Although mothers have the primary duty of providing food for the members of their "kitchen," it is customary for other children to join "kitchen" members other than their own at meal. A child who habitually refuses such hospitality is believed to be acting on the mother's instruction: it is his mother who is therefore to blame. She becomes the target of the gossip of other women, who might instruct their dependents to refuse her meals in retaliation.

The drinking of palm liquor is an important occasion for the Igbo. The palm liquor may be brought by a friend, or by a son-in-law, or it may belong to a kinsman. Other festive occasions for drinking it include marriage, the day for bridewealth payment, the birth of a child, religious rites, the "churching" ceremony of a child and other rites of passage, as well as various meetings of the village associations. Whatever the occasion, everyone is welcome. Visitors are accorded special privileges. Generally, the drinking party shares the same cup (or a few people may share one cup), the titled men being privileged to carry their own gourd cup or horn. Sharing a common cup shows "good feeling," solidarity, and friendship. For members of a drinking party to have their own cups is traditionally looked upon with suspicion because it indicates strained relations and distrust. The dispenser of liquor is required to taste each cupful and to follow a strict order: the host tastes first, then the guests and the visitors; others follow according to seniority and social status.

Hospitality is not restricted to eating and drinking. There is much gift giving and exchanging of farm produce among kinsfolk, in-laws, and friends. Not only are guests provided with food, liquor, and sleeping accommodations; they are given some memorable gifts—seed yams or coco nut seedlings—as a memento of their visit.

"Kola" Hospitality

The sharing of food, meat, and liquor is not as important to the Igbo as the sharing of kola nuts, which play important social and ritual roles in Igbo culture. Traditionally grown to meet social and ritual obligations, *ɔji Igbo* (*cola acuminata*), is less prolific and commercially less important than the less disease-resistant *cola nitida,* which the Igbo call *gworo*—a Hausa word for kola nut.

For social-ritualistic reasons, the Igbo make a distinction between *ɔji ugo* (white kola nut) and *ɔji ɛfu* (kola nut of any other color). *Ɔji ugo* symbolizes luck, "good face," social distinction, and potential prosperity. It is a great honor to be offered *ɔji ugo.* "*Ɔji ugo* comes out," the Igbo say, "when there is a distinguished guest."

Although *ɔji ugo* has such symbolical importance socially, *ɔji aka anɔ* (a four-cotyledon kola nut) is most sought after for ritual reasons. The number four is sacred among Igbo, who have a four-day week. In divination, the number four "count" is auspicious; *ɔfɔ* is struck four times on the ground in any ritual in which it is needed, and in most "parting" sacrifices, the four-path road is an important sacrificial center. It is not surprising, therefore, that the Igbo should accord *ɔji aka anɔ* such a high ritual status.

The kola nut is the greatest symbol of Igbo hospitality. It always comes first. "It is the king." To be presented with a kola nut is to be made welcome; and one is most welcome when the nut turns out "white," whether this is by accident or by design.

Presenting a guest with a kola nut is an important ceremony. Three operations are usually involved: the presentation, the breaking, and the distribution of the kola nut.

It is the host's privilege to present a kola nut, a privilege denied to women (for ritual reasons) and other social inferiors. The host makes this presentation through the next ranking male in his compound or lineage segment. This man reaches the guest through a chain of "relay messengers" who represent differentiated lineage segments. Each person relaying the kola nut recites an appropriate proverb which may set the theme of the gathering or may underscore a previously presented proverb.

When the kola nut finally reaches the principal guest, he completes the relays among his own party and finally sends the kola nut back to his host.

A prayer follows the presentation of the kola nut. The host says the prayer if he is the eldest member of his lineage present. Otherwise, it is the privilege of the eldest person there to say the prayer. A typical prayer calls on the creator, the ancestors, and all friendly spirits to "eat" kola nut. It demands good health, wealth to nourish it, progress for all, and peace to the village. It calls on the wicked and the sorcerers to meet their disastrous end.

The breaking of the kola nut involves the separation of the nut into its various cotyledons. Igbo have two theories which explain the two patterns followed. For the northern Igbo, the breaking of the kola nut is the inalienable right of the host. It must not be delegated to a junior or to a social inferior; for one to do so is to "sell" his elderly status. The southern Igbo think otherwise. In their view, the actual separation of the cotyledons is "service." It may be performed by a junior at the command of his elder or his host. For the guest, his status is incompatible with "sweated" labor. He should not serve his host.

The distribution of the kola nut follows these principles. The host gets the first share, which he eats to demonstrate that it is wholesome and free from poison. The guest and his party then take their shares. Then each member of the host's party gets a share according to the principle of seniority. As each person reaches his share, he dips it into a rich gravy of pepper contained in ɔkwa, a wooden bowl kept specially for eating kola nuts and meat.

The pattern of Igbo hospitality is simple but it is a serious affair. This hospitality cannot be truly evaluated in material terms. It is for the Igbo a matter of great sentiment, around which has grown important rituals. "Kola nut hospitality" demonstrates this. Great travelers themselves, the Igbo know how a guest or a traveler appreciates being made welcome in a "foreign" country.

9

Nonkinship Associations

M ANY SOCIAL and economic associations in Igboland include kin groups in their membership but are not based on the kinship principle. Rather, they are based on the principle of contract or agreement. The life of such associations is terminable at a specified time in the future. The reciprocal rights and obligations of the members are limited to those in the agreement. The membership is open to all qualified persons, the criterion of "qualification" being the potential ability of a prospective member to bear the burden of the agreement. This involves a "moral judgment" and constitutes the noncontractual element found in other contracts. It works in two ways: it makes the membership of a nonkinsman sometimes preferable to that of a kinsman, and vice versa.

Of the various forms of associations and institutions, livestock tenancy was discussed in Chapter 2. The others worth attention here include such economic associations as work groups and credit institutions; and life-membership fraternities, such as the *Dibia* associations and the title-making associations.

Work Groups

Work groups or *onwε ɔru* (exchange of labor) are organized when labor larger than the household unit is required. For prestige farming which the yam title requires, a man needs not only the "right" land resources, but also a regular supply of labor beyond the supply from his household. Although labor can be hired, many Igbo farmers cannot afford it and others think that hiring labor is a waste of money. The cooperative work group remains the chief source of labor supply for such farm operations as bush clearing, planting, and harvest.

Although a work group may recruit its members from its age set, age is not a necessary criterion for membership. An adolescent who can wield a machete may join any work group. The number in a group ranges from two upward. During a farming season a high turnover of membership is typical. Legally, the obligation to perform "return work" is limited to the person who has worked for a farmer and nobody else. For this reason, the membership of a group constantly changes. In actual practice, however, the members of a work group try to ensure that they work for each farmer in turn; when an unforeseen circumstance prevents some members from participating, the work may be postponed to a time when all can be present.

Members of a work group state in advance when they would like to be hosts to the others. There is no official headman as such. Who is the first host is a matter of convenience; the person who organizes others into a work group does so out of self-interest, that is, to enable him to meet his own work obligations. When every member has had his turn, the life of the work group ends and its members may start a new cycle, with new members joining and some of the former members dropping. They may join any other work groups, depending on the individual's farming needs and future commitments. It is through this loosely structured work group that a man meets his labor obligations to his friends in other village-groups (a person may send a work party to his friend without expecting direct payment), to his in-laws, and to his lineage members.

Cooperative work of this kind may take the form of having all the members actually working at the same task, such as bush clearing, or there may be a coordinated division of labor in which different jobs, such as hoeing, planting, and staking yams, are performed by smaller units of the work group. The teamwork involved stimulates competition. The man who works the hardest sets the pace which others follow, each conscious of the efficiency demanded by his group. The slacker, who is usually eliminated during the next cycle, is so demoralized by gossip and "song-making" intended to shame him that he seldom finds a competent work group to join.

Members of the work group are provided lunch, which is taken in the farm. Dinner and other entertainments are held at the host's home. The nightly singing and drumming of the work group are a source of pleasure and attract others, who share the food and other refreshments. The amount of liquor provided governs the amount of singing. A man who keeps his work group singing longest earns the most prestige. Women who serve unappetizing food are satirized and their names mentioned in the songs composed for the occasion.

Credit Associations

While cooperative work groups are indispensable to a "big" Igbo farmer, credit institutions provide ready cash to the trader, to the person who must make a title or a bridewealth payment, to the debtor who must pay his creditor, and to the father who must pay his children's school fees. The Igbo have many names for this institution; *ɔgbɔ, ɔha, isusu, mitiri, compiri,* and *club* (three of these were directly borrowed from English—meeting, club, company), are some of them.

The "contribution club" as these credit institutions are called (Shirley Ardener 1953) provides a form of compulsory saving. It is a system whereby contributors pay a fixed subscription at regular intervals and thus make the fund available to each member in turn. The structure, the organization, the length of time between meetings, and the amount of the take-out share vary with the type of contribution club. However, they share the following common features: A defaulting member, that is, a contributor who fails to make his regular weekly payments, runs the risk of losing all the payments he has hitherto made. If he has claimed his take-out share, he and/or his guarantors are held responsible for the unpaid contribution. Members can accumulate their savings, buy goods on credit, and their membership is sufficient to guarantee short-term or long-term credit facilities from local moneylenders.

The ɔgbɔ system of the contribution club has been well described by Shirley Ardener (1953:129–131) as it operated at Mbaise. According to her report, this ɔgbɔ meets once every eight-day week in a specially constructed hut at the village market. Membership is open to men and women. The weekly subscription for one "hand" (to use the Igbo idiom) is 1 shilling (about 12 cents). This gives a total take-out of £12 8s.—the equivalent of 248 "hands." A person may hold more than one "hand." The body of the membership is controlled by seven headmen called Ndi ishi ɔgbɔ. It is the responsibility of each headman to collect from members subscribing through him, paying for them in case of default and reclaiming from them afterward, sometimes charging a little interest. It is his privilege to decide the order in which his subscribers should receive their take-out, a privilege he manipulates in favor of regular and nondefaulting subscribers.

Once collected, the take-out goes straight to the recipient member, who signs or thumb-prints a receipt and provides a guarantor acceptable to the headmen. For a subscriber with a long history of defaulting this is not an easy matter. If the recipient fails to provide an acceptable guarantor, the take-out is delayed until such a time that one is forthcoming. In one unusual case an acceptable guarantor was not found for three weeks. The would-be recipient of the take-out was by general consensus a defaulting member. The headmen decided to pay him the amount he had collected after they had deducted his debts to the ɔgbɔ. The remaining sum, which was about 45 percent of the total take-out, was retained in the fund and from it the member's remaining subscriptions were made every week. This system of accounting is known locally as "square." The recipient is said to have received his "square" or has "squared" with the ɔgbɔ.

In regular take-out payments, the recipient or, in case of default, his guarantor, is held responsible for his unpaid subscription until every member receives his take-out. Each recipient is obliged to provide six calabashes of palm wine for refreshment and pay 4 shillings into the ɔgbɔ fund from which short-term loans may be made.

At the subscription rate of 1 shilling a week, a take-out of £12 8s. would take 248 Igbo weeks to run its cycle. But by doubling the "hands" every four weeks (a subscriber thus pays 5 shillings in every four Igbo weeks and the ɔgbɔ grants five take-outs) the cycle is reduced to a little over forty-nine Igbo months or approximately four years and eight calendar months. During the life cycle of a contribution club, there are members who are either paying for take-outs already received or for those still due to them.

The importance of the contribution club in Mbaise may be seen from the following data. Ardener reported that six adult men of whom one was receiving a regular wage of 2 pounds a month, one was a fish trader, one a "petty articles" trader, and three worked part time in crafts, were paying among them at least 90 shillings a month, an average of 15 shillings per man. Their total take-outs amounted to £181 7s. 6d., an average of £30 4s. 7d. per man. "Twenty-one . . . women were contributing a known total of £3 8s. 3d. per month, an average of three shillings and three pence towards take-outs amounting to £122 13s., or an average of nearly £5 16s. 10d. per woman" (Ardener 1953:138).

The ɔgbɔ system of contribution clubs places too much power in the hands of a few headmen. Their privilege of nominating for take-outs contributors under them is often abused. A new system developed to deal with this abuse is based on the principle of direct registration and individual responsibility to the club. There are no headmen who control a large body of the total membership.

One of the fairly representative clubs I studied in the Umuahia area has elected officers: chairman, vice-chairman, secretary, treasurer, key holder, police-man, divider, and sanitary inspector. The first five of these officers and seven other members form a committee of twelve, six of whom have actually usurped the decision-making functions of the club, and are an unofficial but a *de facto* inner cabinet. Each member of the club has a number which indicates when his take-out share falls due. This number is his personal property; he can sell it in an open market, lend or lease it to anybody, or abandon it after a cycle of the club.

The club owns a big hall (where it meets) and has two flags. When it is in session, people may walk over but may not ride a bicycle across its premises, and transgression of this rule is punished. It meets every eight-day week—on afɔ day —which is the village market day.

Each "number" pays 2 shillings every eight-day week, and the take-out for that member is £20. Every four weeks the subscription is doubled to enable the "tail" number (as the last one in the register is called) to claim a take-out. Dur-ing the next double subscription, the middle number claims a take-out. In effect, one of the double take-outs rotates between the tail number and the middle num-ber. Although the monthly doubling appears to shorten the life of the club by forty Igbo weeks (these are eight-day weeks), this is actually not so. The club provides itself with a fund by claiming all the first eight take-outs at the begin-ning of each cycle. This amounts to exactly £160. From this fund loans are made to members at interest rate of 100 percent, payment being made when the take-outs of these debtors fall due. (This area charges interest in a very curious way. Loans repaid after six months carry an interest rate of 200 percent, but no further interest is charged even if the loan is not repaid for many years.) The fund serves another important function: it stabilizes the membership of the club. Since its earnings are not usually shared after each club cycle, this tends to make the contributors loyal to their club.

A person who claims a take-out spends about 10 shillings (or 2.5 percent of the take-out) in providing refreshments—raphia liquor and meat—the latter being shared equally among the "numbers." He signs or thumb-prints an agreement and provides a guarantor, who may be his wife, his son, or a relative. Then he collects his take-out after paying any debts to the club.

Clubs of this type are often organized by professional or trade groups— teachers, tailors, traders, tinkers, and government and local council employees. The members usually pay a higher rate of subscription at monthly intervals. In some cases, the life of their club is limited to a calendar year. They operate a most economical club system: there is no "standing" fund, and no loans are made. There may not be any entertainment expenses.

Another type of contribution club is known as the women's *mitiri*. Though run by women, the membership of the women's *mitiri* is open to both men and women. Their "clubs have a reputation for being very strictly organized, no latitude being given to defaulters. On the other hand, it is maintained that head women do not, as a rule, demand unofficial payments from recipients" (Ardener, 1953: 133).

Two types of women's *mitiri* may be distinguished: the *ɔgbɔ* system and the "target fund" system. The organization, structure, and operations of the former have been discussed. The target fund has the following peculiar characteristics. The take-out is not paid out weekly but is shared annually to meet a specific need, such as to buy clothes for a ceremony, to provide funds for a local Christmas feast. (Christmas feasts are scheduled to fall on the village market-day so as to enable relatives in other village-groups to attend.) The meeting takes place in the compound of each member in turn. "Church women" may organize this type of club to enable them to pay their church dues. Ɵmɵ-ckpɵ (women married outside their own village) use such an association as a means of "knowing themselves" and of taking collective action in such matters as funerals, second burial ceremonies, and weddings in their natal villages that they must attend.

The amount of weekly subscription varies from 1 penny to 6 pence a week. The fund is lent out to members or those sponsored by them at the interest rate of 1 penny per shilling per week. The capital borrowed is required to be "shown" to the club each week as evidence of "credit-worthiness." The increase to the fund at such a high rate of interest can be appreciated from the fact that one small club of twenty-three members had accumulated a total of £3 14s. "Just over a year later this fund was worth £17 19s. 4-½d., an increase of approximately 459%" (Ardener 1953:135).

Whatever their form, contribution clubs serve many functions in Igboland, one of which is the encouragement of thrift. An adolescent boy who shows some signs of being wasteful is forced to join an *ɔgbɔ*, where he is compelled to save. A member of a contribution club can sign over rights to his take-outs in order to borrow cash, raise trading capital, or buy goods on credit. With his take-outs, he

can make bridewealth payments, lease land, take titles (another form of investment), become a village moneylender, or provide second burial feasts for his deceased parents. The weekly meetings are a valuable form of social gathering. The
contribution clubs themselves are the mainstay of such other institutions and associations as the *Dibia* fraternities and the title-making societies. It is doubtful
whether many Igbo would be able to finance the costly titles they take without
this form of credit institution.

Dibia Associations

From the consideration of credit institutions, we come to other forms of
associations which confer life membership and provide insurance for their members. *Mitiri dibia,* as the association of all ordained priests in a village-group is
called, is an example. The main function of the association is to lay down and
enforce the rules which govern the operations of the *dibia* (medicine men). It is
through the respect for their laws that they safeguard their economic interests.
Because of the Igbo respect for their *dibia,* a fact reflected in the many immunities they enjoy, members of the *dibia* fraternity were among the most traveled
Igbo in pre-British days. They exploited their immunities to the full, and were
able to establish a Pan-Igbo solidarity even in the days when travel within Igbo
country was considered dangerous.

"*Dibia*" is a word the Igbo tend to use loosely. A herbalist, a diviner, or a
medicine man may be referred to as *dibia.* But the membership of *mitiri dibia* is
not open to all of them. In this limited reference, a *dibia* is one who has performed "*igwɔ ajá*"—the rite of ordination. This rite confers on the initiate all
priestly functions. Whether he practices or not is irrelevant. Through ordination,
a *dibia* acquires the power to "see things"—the power of "vision" (ɵhɵ). Since
he "sees things," he can divine, but most of them choose not to do so. Ordination does not necessarily confer the knowledge of herbs. It is knowledge which
can be acquired by anybody at a price. In fact, a reputable herbalist may not be an
ordained priest. There is a great contrast between the solidarity among the *dibia*
and the competition and open rivalry among herbalists. Probably the competitive
nature of the latter's profession and the temperament of their Igbo clients, who
expect a herbalist to cure their illness in a few days or face competition from
other herbalists, account for this.

The *mitiri dibia* recruits its members through ordination. This is usually a
very costly ritual ceremony lasting for about eight days, during which time the
initiate is secluded and "doctored" with medicine. He pays a high initiation fee
which is shared equally among members. It is from this fee that members recover
the cost of their own initiation. Seniority in the *mitiri dibia* is based on the order
of initiation and not on age order. It is in the same order that "shares" are taken.
Although some *mitiri dibia* organize contribution clubs for their members, this is
not an important function for them. Unlike some of the recent associations, the
mitiri dibia is still run on traditional lines. There are few elected offices, though
the treasurer and the "key holders" (usually two officers drawn from different vil-

lages) are becoming important. They still meet at the homes of each member in turn. The host provides some refreshments including food, meat, and palm wine.

Title Societies

Like the *dibia* associations, membership in the title-making societies and the secret societies is for life. The title-taker and the initiate in the secret society pay a heavy initiation fee which is shared equally among members, the sharing following the order of initiation. In effect, these associations serve as mutual insurance societies, enabling the socially ambitious to invest the savings he accumulated in his youth while guaranteeing him continued economic support and prestige during his old age. It provides him with a Pan-Igbo passport which he carries with him, a passport which guarantees him all perquisites and accords him a place of honor and dignity among "foreign" associations which would otherwise give him a hostile reception. The associations exercise a form of social control by laying down certain rules of conduct for their members and proscribing certain forms of behavior which are considered unworthy of a titled man. Even today, these associations have not outlived their usefulness, nor have they lost their appeal to the people. "The retiring official or professional man may know a great deal about the outside world, but he lacks any detailed knowledge of the politics of the little village world which he now wishes to influence; and membership in the local societies brings him into intimate and friendly contact with those men who have spent their lives mastering this particular subject" (Jones, 1956: 23).

Associations and Village Integration

The various forms of associations described here cut across village and village-group boundaries. They help in intervillage integration and communication. Work groups, for instance, operate far beyond their village-group in order "to return work" to some members, or to help out friends and patrons. The itinerant work groups often create other ties, such as trading partnerships, marriage alliances, and exchanges of local judges. (It is common practice for the Igbo to "hire" the services of judges outside their village to help represent them.)

In the same way, contribution clubs increase their members' range of contact and facilitate the lending and borrowing of money among village-groups. After his own village and his mother's natal village, the next village the Igbo boy comes to know is the village where his parents pay their weekly subscription. Until he becomes well known, this is a "hostile" village in which he expects to be challenged by boys of his age. There he cannot back out of a "fair" fight (fighting with a boy of his own age), nor can he plead the possibility of being attacked as an excuse for not running his father's errands in the villages. To face challengers without fear is one of the ways of growing up. If he successfully defends himself or, better, puts other boys on the defensive, the boy will make lasting friendships in this village and the others will begin to respect him for his courage.

Whereas work groups and contribution clubs promote local and regional integration, the *dibia* and the title-making associations aid Pan-Igbo integration. They confer on their members a Pan-Igbo citizenship, while, paradoxically, they remain organizationally local. Every Igbo respects a titled man, no matter what area he comes from. His identification presents no problem. His bearing and his brass-bound iron spear, together with the red camwood cords or ivory rings around his ankles, are sufficient indicators of a titled status. For the *dibia,* a cautious gait, a smoke-stained bag hanging over one shoulder, and chalk-marked eye lids are badges of his profession.

10

Status Placement among Igbo

THE PHRASE "status placement" refers to the generally accepted position an individual occupies in his society. A system of social status therefore implies two major principles of stratification: a common basis of ranking, and a hierarchical order. In describing the status placement among them, I shall try to make clear how the Igbo conceptualize their ranking arrangement through the application of the above principles.

In most ethnographic literature the image of the Igbo is that of an egalitarian society in which almost everybody is equal. This picture obscures the regional differences in Igbo social structure, and often results from the confusion of Igbo ideology with the reality of their social placement of individuals. Structurally, there are marked differences in the political organizations of different Igbo village-groups: an elective monarchy in the Onitsha community, a divinely ordained king in the Nri community, for example. And in the village-group of Nike, in northeast Igbo, there are still some slave communities, a very atypical structure for Igbo. In spite of these differences, all Igbo share the same equalitarian ideology: the right of the individual to climb to the top, and faith in his ability to do so.

Age and Kinship Status

One of the ways of approaching Igbo status placement is through the kinship system, that is, treating kinship as a network of interrelated statuses. The important features of Igbo kinship include precedence accorded to the male, seniority by birth order irrespective of sex, emphasis on agnation, the polygynous household, and virilocal residence. Seniority by birth order is the normal basis for ɔpara status (extended family headship), the investment of ɔfɔ—the symbol of ritual authority of ɔpara and other heads of lineages as well as other male-linked offices and positions.

A typical Igbo village-group consists of a number of semiautonomous villages, each of which is segmented into ɵmɵnna groups (patrilineages). Each ɵmɵnna group is territorially distinguished from similar ɵmɵnna groups and is symbolically referred to as ama—a path (for example, Ama ɵmɵ Nga—"The path of the children of Nga"). At the head of the ɵmɵnna group is ɔpara, the oldest ranking male who holds the lineage ɔfɔ. Ɵmɵnna as a territorial unit is physically divided into a number of ɛzi—large dwelling units, each having a common, roomy lounge called ovu. The oldest male is the onyɛ nwɛ ɛzi—the compound head. Within each ɛzi are clustered huts and/or modern bungalows (reflecting the economic status of their owners) belonging to members of different domestic groups. The head of each domestic group exercises authority roles over its members, who, in turn, can appeal to the compound head if they feel they have been unjustly treated. In effect, ɛzi can be conceptualized as a number of domestic units physically united by a common ovu and jurally controlled by a compound head who intervenes in their internal conflicts and handles their external affairs. Symbolically, one ovu is equivalent to one compound, which in turn is a small segment of an ɵmɵnna group, the effective social organizational structure of an Igbo village.

In the Igbo compound, as in all Igbo society, seniority by age regulates social placement. Two age positions are formally institutionalized—ɔpara and ada. Ɔpara status is accorded to the first male child and ada status to the first female child of a man, irrespective of the age or co-wife order of their mothers. These children occupy very important and responsible social positions in the family. The behavior between kinsmen and nonkinsmen is regulated by the seniority-juniority principle. The seniors are the moral agents of the young. It is the duty of children to greet their seniors first in the morning or whenever they meet. In children's play groups, leadership and authority are informally vested in the older boys and girls. Among children of the same mother and among children of the same father but of different mothers and different age grades, the principle of "sharing by birth order" is followed—a procedure that tends to preserve the ranking by birth order. In one context, the distinction between child and adult superficially overrides other status considerations in Igbo society. An Igbo child remains a child, no matter what his other status distinctions are. His senior who is less distinguished socially loses no time in reminding him of his age.

Besides age, affinal relationship creates a very important status position for one's children. This is the okɛlɛ (okɛnɛ that is, okɛ nnɛ—great mother) status. Every Igbo individual is accorded okɛlɛ status in his umunɛ—his mother's lineage. It is here that he becomes a most welcome honorary member. His person is considered sacred. His umunɛ supports him against his ɵmɵnna and should he be convicted of sorcery, his only place of exile is his umunɛ.

Marriage and Social Position

Married status is an important variable in the status configuration of the Igbo. Married life is the normal condition for adults, and polygyny for the men is the ideal, being an important status indicator. The Igbo who remains single does so not out of choice but because of economic necessity: the inability to provide the bridewealth payment. The unmarried adult male is referred to as *okɛ okporo* (male woman), a pejorative term, while the unmarried woman is referred to by a descriptive phrase—*Onwɛgh di* ("She has no husband"). Widows are referred to as *ishi nkpɛ* ("Mourning head") and form part of the marriageable population. Igbo is a society which has no concept of celibacy but tolerates celibates as victims of economic forces.

Polygyny has obvious status implications for the common husband and his co-wives. Igbo women support and often even finance polygyny because it enhances their social status and lightens their domestic chores, thus giving them the much-needed leisure to do their private trading. With a co-wife, the first wife assumes the coveted status of *nnɛkwu* ("The big mother"). Other co-wives are ranked in seniority according to their marriage order to the common husband. In this marriage-order ranking, age, wealth, fertility, positions, and prospects of offspring of the co-wife are not factors. They are, nevertheless, important status variables, especially in the interpersonal and extrafamilial relations of the co-wives concerned. In the wider Igbo society, those variables may take precedence over the marriage order. A woman may be highly ranked because of the position of a distinguished son, her success in trading, or her position in the women's title society, irrespective of her marriage order. Indeed, some women are ranked higher than their husbands because of their distinctions in other spheres. Wealthy women marry in their own right, found big compounds, and play the role of social father quite effectively.

Polygyny has its tensions. The interests of a husband often conflict with those of his wives. Women tend to exclude men from their leisure activities. Their virilocal residence after marriage and other sex-linked roles tend to create a distinct sex subculture. A husband is often a victim of concerted action by his wives, an action that might force him into submission. This situation may be ameliorated by the *nwanyimma,* the love wife. She remains the confidante of the husband and enjoys a special status, but she is also a target of abuse and gossip by other co-wives.

The Status of Women

The women members of an Igbo village are of two categories: the *ɵmɵɔkpɵ*, who may be unmarried, married, divorced, or widowed women who belong to the village by descent, and the *ndom alɵ alɵ* who belong to it by marriage. The rule that women should always be married gives marriage the precedence over descent. The relation between these two classes of women is one of "potential" conflict covertly expressed in the joking relationship between them and overtly manifested in the institutionalized authority of the ɘmɘɔkpɘ over the *ndom alɘ alɘ* during the mourning rites marking the latter's widowhood.

Today, the impact of European culture affects the form of marriage and the consequent status placement of women. Igbo marriages can be classified as traditional marriage, church marriage, and civil marriage. All these marriage forms are validated by the payment of bridewealth. The two innovations in present-day Igbo marriages—church marriage and civil marriage—have their foundation on the traditional form. Whether the final rituals of marriage are performed in the church or in the court registrar's office, the marriage must begin with two families—the family of the bride and that of the bridegroom. By consensus, church marriage commands the highest prestige. This is followed by civil marriage and then the traditional form. Civil marriage is usually preferred by educated men and women who do not put much value on church membership. Associated with the new marriage forms is the title *Misisi*—the Igbo rendering for "Mrs." It is the aspiration of all Igbo women who value the associational status conferred by church membership to "marry in Church" and thus be privileged to be addressed as *Misisi*.

The African woman regarded as a chattel of her husband, who has made a bridewealth payment on her account, is not an Igbo woman, who enjoys a high socioeconomic and legal status. She can leave her husband at will, abandon him if he becomes a thief, and summon him to a tribunal, where she will get a fair hearing. She marries in her own right and manages her trading capital and her profits as she sees fit. Though women are not the normal instrument through which land rights are passed, and though their virilocal residence after marriage makes it impossible for them to play some important social and ritual roles in their natal village, yet they can have leasehold, take titles, and practice medicine.

Diala and Non-Diala Status

Besides the differences in the masculine and feminine status placement discussed, the most important distinction the Igbo make in their stratification system is that between *Diala* and non-*Diala*. The *Diala* is a freeborn. One of the first things a stranger learns in an Igbo community is the importance of this distinction. It divides Igbo society into two clearly defined social strata; the non-*Diala* being subordinate to the *Diala*.

In spite of its clear status reference, the *Diala*–non-*Diala* dichotomy is weak for many reasons. It treats each group as homogeneous, when in fact each is highly differentiated. It ignores such important status positions as those of leaders, priests, slaves, cult-slaves, pawns, and strangers. It neglects the economic factor crucial in the Igbo system of stratification. By creating an illusory antithesis, it oversimplifies Igbo social structure. Rather than follow this dual model, I shall discuss the status positions found in Igbo society, such as *Diala, Osu, Ohu,* and the various forms of leadership and occupational statuses, and see what combination of status variables is in operation.

Diala is a freeborn, full citizen. As described in chapter 6, his status is symbolized by the burial of his navel cord, preferably at the foot of an oil palm tree. To be a *Diala* is to have the doors of title societies and other institutions open to one. The only barrier to social climbing is economic: the payment of the membership fees. The *Diala* is accorded a high social and ritual status, regardless of his age, sex, or wealth.

In contrast to the *Diala,* the *Ohu* was a slave. Slaving and slavery had a long history in Igboland. Slaves were the victims either of intergroup wars or of economic circumstances. They may have been captured, kidnaped, or sold to meet pressing indebtedness. Although slaves had few rights, and their treatment varied with the character of their masters, there is every indication that generally Igbo treated their slaves well. "Not infrequently, a slave became the companion of his master and is put in a position demanding great trustworthiness" (Basden 1921: 109). Slaves were generally absorbed into the lineage of their masters, the only exception to this pattern being at Nike (a northern Igbo village-group) where "slave communities" are reported (Horton, 1954: 311–336). With the absorption of slaves into the master's lineage, it became taboo to mention the fact of their origin.

Although a slave could marry the master's daughter and some slave women were married by their masters, a slave was not allowed to sacrifice to *ala*—the earth-goddess. This is the privilege of a *Diala*. This was not a great disability since strangers are by definition excluded from this ritual privilege even though their *Diala* status is acknowledged by all.

Pawns are distinguished from slaves. The Igbo make fine status distinctions between the two. As they conceive their statuses, a slave was a man whose links with his lineage had been severed forever. This is not true of a pawn. Although slaves could be sold for cash, given in payment for a debt, or simply handed over to a new master in anticipation of a favor, no such fate faces a pawn. Slaves and pawns are referred to by a generic term, *ohu,* but pawns are often terminologically distinguished from slaves by a descriptive term—*nvuvu akɵ* (collateral for wealth). Before the introduction of all-purpose money into Ibgoland, pawns were collateral for cows, horses, expensive ivory ornaments, and other items needed for title-taking and second-burial rites—*ɔkwukwu.* It was considered legitimate and perfectly respectable for a man to pawn himself in order to raise the bridewealth payment for a wife. When his creditor-master was a villager, the pawn was expected to live in his house while meeting his work obligation; if the creditor-master lived in another village, the pawn was required to take up residence with him. For the pawn, the change in status is dramatic: from *okɛ okporo* status—bachelor status—to a married pawn. That such cases occur indicates what prestige married status enjoys in Igbo society.

Pawns have special privileges and obligations. They cannot be repawned by a creditor-master. Their death does not terminate their obligations; rather, their sureties are held responsible. Usually they work for the creditor-master for a definite number of days in an Igbo week as specified in the contract. For the remaining days in the week, they work as craftsmen or as laborers to earn their redemption money.

Pawning is not yet dead in Igboland, though coresidence of a pawn with his creditor-master has almost disappeared. There is evidence that the pawning of young girls is still going on despite government disapproval.

The Osu System of Slavery

Osu is a cult-slave, a slave who has been dedicated to the service of the dedicator's deity. The descendants of such a cult-slave are also *osu*. The dedicator may be an individual, an extended family, or a lineage. Neither a *Diala,* nor an *Ohu,* nor a pawn is *Osu*. To refer to them as *osu* is the gravest of all insults.

The *osu* system of slavery constitutes the greatest contradiction to Igbo equalitarian ideology. *Osu* are a people with a status dilemma: a people hated and despised yet indispensable in their ritual roles; a people whose achievements are spurned by a society which is aggressively achievement-oriented. Although *osu* function as "special" priests, they are not accorded the high status other priests who are "general practitioners" enjoy. Rather, "the *osu* are hated and feared, treated as if mean and discussed with the tone of horror and contempt" (Leith-Ross 1937: 206).

The *osu* system of slavery seems to have originated within, and diffused from the Owerri-Okigwi region, its largest zone of persistence. It has not yet diffused into northeastern Igbo or into Umuahia-Ngwa in the southeast. Probably Ngwa dispersal from Mbaise predates its diffusion into that area. There is a correlation between the powerful oracles of central Igbo—*Igwɛka-Ala* of Umunoha in Owerri, *Amadi-ɔha* (Kamalu) of Ozuzu in Ikwerre, and *Agbara* of Awka—and the incidence of *osu*. The pronouncements of these oracles in regard to sacrificial or ritual procedures were seldom neglected, even if they called for the use of human beings.

The various traditions of *osu* origin point to its essentially religious basis. Although the *osu* tradition claims that their ancestors were pro-Aro priests who were highly respected until they were supplanted, the *diala* tradition is a scapegoat theory. In that view, a village, a lineage, a family, or an individual dogged by illness, bad luck, or calamities and misfortunes would consult a diviner to find out what was wrong. In such a case, the diviner would recommend the dedication of a slave who would then become the deity's servitor and carry the sins of the dedicator. Such a servitor became an *osu*. He is feared because the *diala* do not know how to interact with him without offending the deity. He is hated because the *osu* remind the *diala* of their guilt.

The *osu* system finds rationalization in Igbo religious belief and dogma. The Igbo believe that to fall out of favor with the deities is to lose ritual status—a state of uncleanliness that can be purged by the sacrificial lamb, which in this case happened to be a human being. The social isolation of the *osu* is intended to safeguard the community from further ritual contamination and complications.

Since nobody is sure of the acceptable form of interaction with the *osu,* only ritual interaction, such as participation in sacrifices, sanctioned by a diviner is tolerated.

The cult-slave status of the *osu* was legally abolished by the Eastern Nigerian Government in 1956. Before this date, acculturation had dealt a serious blow to this form of slavery. The degrading marks of mutilation which *diala* tradition claims were the physical marks of the *osu* (tradition claims that the *osu* were deliberately deformed to distinguish them from *diala*) belonged to a barbaric past, if they ever occurred. The privileged marketing which forbade *diala* to buy seed yams from *osu;* the practice of not sharing a barber, drinking cups, or the same farm locations with *osu,* and exclusive right of grave burial for the *diala* are privileges which could not be maintained in a rapidly changing society.

Although legally abolished, the *osu* system is not dead. In a descending order of ascribed status, Igbo still distinguish *diala, ohu,* and *osu.* The *osu* lineages are still a living social reality; their residential segregation has not been abolished by law. In Orlu and Okigwi, homesteads near the village markets generally belong to *osu.* This residential pattern grew up when *osu* were subsisting on public charity. There is no generally acknowledged intermarriage or willingness to intermarry between *diala* and *osu,* even among the most acculturated Igbo. However, sexual relations which were tabooed between the two groups do occur, especially in cities.

Paradoxically, the social disabilities of the *osu* are the sources of their ritual privileges and legal protection. Unlike slaves, they cannot be absorbed into their master's lineage; on the other hand, they are protected by their deity from being sold or killed, or expropriated. They are not economically exploited. Denied traditional status, the *osu* were among the first Igbo to accept Western education, religious ideas, and other economic opportunities. They are today found among the best educated and the wealthiest Igbo, but unfortunately, others are still silent about their great achievements.

Leadership and Status Placement

From the consideration of the *osu,* who are priests without power and prestige, we come to the groups of individuals who command both. In translating the power relations in Igbo society into status terms, it is more appropriate to speak of leaders and their supporters rather than of rulers and their subjects. We have indicated earlier that the kingship institutions found among some Igbo communiies are intrusive traits which have not diffused beyond the territories of their immigrant bearers. Even among such communities, there is no ruling class as such and the term "chief" or "king" used in the sense of an executive authority, or the person from whom such authority derives, cannot be applied.

The Igbo pattern of leadership is one in which the secular-ritual roles are combined. Leaders are essentially "opinion" leaders. They must be sensitive to public opinion and embody what is the best in Igbo tradition. Ɔfɔ holders meet this criterion; hence their social importance. Ɔfɔ is the symbol of authority. Its physical representation is a piece of wood from *Detarium elastica,* and a functioning *ɔfɔ* resembles a club. The *ɔpara* of the lineage holds the big *ɔfɔ* while the smaller ones are held by the senior males of the minor lineages. The distribution of *ɔfɔ* among the various segments shows that ritual and secular authority among the Igbo is not unified but evenly distributed.

A devout *ɔfɔ* holder says his daily prayers with his *ɔfɔ* placed on the ground. He is the medium between the living lineage members and the ancestors. He sacrifices to *ala*—the earth-goddess—on behalf of his patrilineage, brings his *ɔfɔ* when people are to be sworn by the town, and participates in the legislative, executive, and judicial activities of the villages.

Whereas the *ɔfɔ* holders lead because of the politico-religious sanctions attached to their office, the titled men are given more secular roles. A rigid distinction between titled men and *ɔfɔ* holders cannot be made. A fairly accurate generalization is that all titled positions are achieved but that all *ɔfɔ* positions are assigned. On the other hand, the Igbo title system defies generalization. It varies from the hierarchical *Ndichiɛ* system of Onitsha and *Oguta,* the *Ɔzɔ* system of Onitsha, Oguta, Nri, and Okigwi, through the less structured *Ndiama* system of the Nsukka area to the *Ɔkɔnkɔ-ɛzɛji* systems of the Owerri, Okigwi, Orlu, Umuahia, and Ngwa communities. With all its variations in structure and content, the Igbo title system shares the following common characteristics. It institutionalizes natural leadership. All the title societies which have survived contact with Western culture involve the expenditure of wealth, which is the admission fee. It provides an important criterion for measuring prestige. A person's title "pecking order" indicates his prestige; his membership in a title society indicates his social status.

Associational Status

Agriculture is the basic Igbo industry. People whose yam houses are full, and who have taken the yam title (*ɛzɛji*), command great prestige. It is the *ɛzɛji* who are privileged to have, by the pronouncement of diviners, the yam-oriented male and female children called *Njɔku* and *Mmaji,* respectively. *Njɔku* and *Mmaji* occupy a distinct ritual status. *Mmaji* must be the first wife of her husband as well as the only wife with her ascribed status. The Igbo have developed an ambivalent attitude toward *Mmaji* and *Njɔku.* They are loved as "status objects" but hated for the problems they create at their death, which puts a taboo on yams. No member of the family may eat yam until they are ritually buried—a very costly affair. "A *Njɔku* or *Mmaji* who is today literate must find a female or male opposite to marry. Though a Christian, he is forced by his culture, and often by fear, to owe allegiance to two worlds— the traditional religion and the Christian faith" (Uchendu 1964a:32).

When we consider other occupations than farming we see that Igbo exhibit many regional specializations. There are the famous blacksmiths of Awka and Nkwerri, the priest-chiefs of Nri, the fishermen-farmers of Oguta, and the cloth weavers of Akwete. European contact has led to the multiplication of occupational roles among the Igbo. Unfortunately, occupational ranking, which is an attractive model for status placement, faces two major difficulties when applied to the Igbo. In the first place, traditionally the people are ideologically opposed to occupational ranking. It is their prayer that "whatever a man's occupation, may it provide for his old age." Second, most people pursue several occupations simultaneously. A person may be a farmer, a trader, a doctor, and a drummer simultaneously. This makes consensus in occupational ranking difficult to attain.

The Igbo model for viewing their social stratification is based on wealth. It does not matter what occupations a person engages in "to provide for his old age." With this ideological rather than an analytical model, they distinguish between *ogbɛnyɛ* or *mbi*—the poor—from *dinkpa*—the moderately prosperous—and the latter from *nnukwu madu* or *ɔgaranya*—the rich. This classification still ignores the widespread practice of occupational combination, the *diala-osu* dichotomy, the chief sources of wealth—whether from farming, trading, or medicine—as well as other kinship variables which affect status placement. Its chief utility lies in the fact that it commands general consensus and provides a normative frame which guides behavior.

Western Impact on the Igbo Status System

Igbo is a society in which the old and the new coexist, and the one modifies the other in order to make this coexistence possible. The church, the school, the city, and politics have all created new statuses. The church has produced indigenous bishops, priests, and a hierarchy of church elders; the school has various grades of teachers distinguished by professional training, salaries, and varying consumption patterns and social expectations. The city has brought about a rural-urban distinction marked by differences in role-specialization. Merchants, petty traders, clerks, and migrant laborers are among the important status positions in the cities. In politics, we have a whole hierarchy of statuses in which ministers of state, parliamentarians, the traditional and the "new" chiefs, and, at the local government level, the councilors occupy the most important positions.

The data presented here show how complex the status structure of Igbo society is when approached analytically. There is no one status model which will not oversimplify this structure. The occupational model, a very useful one for Western societies, hides more than it reveals when applied to Igbo society. As has been made clear, most Igbo derive their income from more than one occupation; the specialized roles providing one source of income are new, the result of acculturation. The wealth-prestige model appears to be the only status model that is coextensive with Igbo society. The Igbo make clear distinctions between wealth (*akɵ, ɵba*), status position (*ɔkwa*), and prestige (*ɵdɵ*). They stress wealth and prestige in status placement, a stress that makes individual achievement primary and defines social mobility in wealth-prestige terms. In this way, the Igbo treat wealth and prestige as two different variables. The *osu* may be wealthy but they command no prestige. A person impoverished by costly title taking, or whose title-taking fee is paid by a junior wealthy relative, may have no wealth but commands much prestige. The Igbo "big" man, whether a politician, a college professor, a chief, a merchant, or a company director may be wealthy, but his prestige depends on how he "converts" his wealth into prestigious acts: taking a title, owning a country house, providing his relations with a college education, and donating generously to his town's scholarship or to the development fund are the modern ways of converting wealth into prestige.

11

Igbo Gods and Oracles

THE IGBO ARE a religious people. Their belief system and an elaborate religious worship organized around it confirm this. Although Igbo religious beliefs have not been systematized into a body of dogma, the following striking aspects of their religion may be noted. It is a tribal religion in the sense that its major tenets are shared by all Igbo-speaking people, but in matters of religious participation, it remains organizationally local, the most effective unit of religious worship being the extended family. Periodic rituals and ceremonies may activate the lineage or the village-group, the latter being the widest political community. Second, it is a polytheistic religion; their numerous deities, which are strikingly democratic, continue to increase with the rate of culture contact. Although the minor deities are highly competitive, each still retains its sphere of independent activity and power over the living and may solicit the living for servitors. Finally, religion rationalizes the individual's ability to improve his status either in the world of man or after his reincarnation, in the world of the ancestors. This is a dynamic factor in Igbo receptivity to change.

Igbo Ideas of the High God

The idea of a creator of all things is focal to Igbo theology. They believe in a supreme god, a high god, who is all good. The logical implication of the concept of a god who is all good is the existence of a devil (*agbara*) to whom all evil must be attributed. This is not peculiar to Igbo thought. It is a characteristic of all known religions which accept the doctrine of a high god who does no evil.

The Igbo high god is a withdrawn god. He is a god who has finished all active works of creation and keeps watch over his creatures from a distance. The Igbo high god is not worshiped directly. There is neither shrine nor priest dedicated to his service. He gets no direct sacrifice from the living but is conceived as the ultimate receiver of all sacrifice made to the minor deities. (In fact, Igbo sacrifice to any unknown and uninvited deities who might be present.) He seldom interferes in the affairs of men, a characteristic which sets him apart from all other deities, spirits, and ancestors. He is a satisfied god who is not jealous of the prosperity of man on earth.

Although the Igbo feel psychologically separated from their high god, he is not too far away, he can be reached, but not as quickly as can other deities who must render their services to man to justify their demand for sacrifices. The Igbo recognize that the high god can do all things. It is their experience, too, that he lets the minor, malignant deities torture them, rob them of their property, kill their children, and make trade unprofitable and women and land barren and unproductive. Their appeals to him at the height of their distress and despondency do not always meet with immediate response. Is it any wonder that they sometimes feel that the distance between them and the high god is too great? Although the high god may be distant and withdrawn, he is not completely separated from the affairs of men. He is still the great father, the source of all good. He interacts with each Igbo during each reincarnation cycle. He sometimes intervenes in favor of the living but not as quickly as suppliants would like.

The high god is conceived of in different roles. In his creative role, he is called *Chinɛkɛ, Chi-Okikɛ* (*Chi*—God; *Okikɛ*—that creates). To distinguish him from other minor gods he is called *Chukwu*—the great or the high god. As the creator of everything, he is called *Chukwu Abiama,* while as the pillar that supports the heavens, he is called *Agalaba ji igwɛ.* The sky is regarded as his place of residence and people invoke his name as *Chi-di-n'ɛlu*—"God who lives above."

Besides the high god, there are other minor gods called nature gods, sometimes described as kind, hospitable and industrious; at other times, they are conceived of as fraudulent, treacherous, unmerciful, and envious. They are, in general, subject to human passions and weaknesses. But they can be controlled, manipulated, and, in fact, used to further human interests.

The organization and power structure of these nature gods mirror Igbo social structure. Like the latter, the nature gods are not conceived of as forming a hierarchical pantheon. There is no seniority or authority implied in the conception of these minor deities. Though some gods are conceived of as being more uncompromising and more wicked than others, yet this trait does not make them rank higher or lower than the other deities. It is the Igbo practice to appeal to one god or to a number of gods simultaneously without any consideration of their rank or status. The Igbo demand from their gods effective service and effective protection. If they fail in this duty, they are always threatened with starvation and desertion. Given effective protection, the Igbo are very faithful to their gods.

Ala, the Earth-Goddess

Though the minor gods are not normally ranked in importance the Igbo regard *ala,* the earth-goddess, nearest to them, with the possible exception of their ancestors. *Ala* is an earth-goddess, a great mother. She is the spirit of fertility. She increases the fertility of man and the productivity of the land. Without her, life would be impossible for the Igbo, who attach much sentiment to the land. It is out of respect to the earth-goddess that the Igbo are ideologically opposed to the sale of land. As was noted earlier, where there is a "sale" of land the earth-goddess must be ritually pacified if the transaction is to be consummated. The Igbo feel guilty and ashamed to have to sell their land.

Every Igbo community has a myth about its settlement—a myth which validates its claim to the piece of land it inhabits. Some villagers claim that their founding parents were created on the spot; others lay claim to priority of settlement. Whatever the basis of the charter, the first settlers are always said to have founded *ihu ala*—the face of the earth—which thus becomes sacred for the people. *Ihu Ala* is the place where all major decisions, like going to war, summarily dispatching a sorcerer, or giving a democratically reached decision a ritual binder, are made. The Igbo are fond of changing their mind, but decisions taken at *ihu ala* are not lightly treated and are often respected.

Ala is a merciful mother. She intercedes for her children with other spirits. Minor deities may not take action against Igbo without asking *ala* to "warn" her children, but no spirit may intercede or intervene when *ala* has decided to punish. But she does not punish in haste; she gives many signals of her displeasure. Quite reluctantly, after many unheeded warnings, *ala* may kill by bouncing the wicked on the ground until they are dead. She does not kill for minor offenses. Only such offenses classed as *nsọ—alǝ* (*taboo*)—warrant her anger. Incest is a good example. As the custodian of Igbo morality, *ala* must take action to save the community. Death is not considered enough punishment for an Igbo who has offended against *ala*. He is denied ground burial, the worst social humiliation for any Igbo.

Ala helps the Igbo with many things. They ask her for children, for prosperity in trade, and for increase in livestock. As the source of strength, she must be notified before her children go to war. It is a great privilege to be a priest of *ala*. This requires a *diala*-status, which is ascribed to all children born of a freeman and a freewoman. Every *diala* is therefore a potential priest of *ala*.

Other Spirits

Anyanwu is the sun-god. He makes crops and trees grow. Igbo distinguish between the physical phenomena of the sun and its spiritual aspects. The spiritual aspects are called *kamalu* or *amadịọha*—the lightning spirit. The latter is distinguished from lightning, called *amǝma*. *Amadịọha* lives in the sun. His voice is manifested in lightning and heard in thunder. Generally, every Igbo community recognizes the existence of *kamalu* (*Amadịọha*), but its worship is usually the affair of a lineage or lineage segment. Such a lineage or lineage segment has the prerogative of appointing a priest who ministers to the needs of other people needing the service of the deity. Ọ*zuzu*, a southern Igbo village-group, has developed a most powerful oracle called *kamalu ọzuzu*. We shall hear more about its influence and operations later. Children born on *afɔ* (the second day of the Igbo four-day week) are named *Anyanwu* if this status is confirmed by divination. There is no special ritual role attached to this name. It appears that such names simply remind the Igbo that those named after the *anyanwu* deity were conceived at the deity's intervention. It is the Igbo belief that gods "escort" children (*ihita nwa*) to a couple needing them.

Igwɛ is the sky-god. Igbo believe that the sky is larger than the earth; hence the name *igwɛ k'ala*. *Igwɛ* is the source of rain, but it is seldom appealed to for rain. Rather, rain makers claim the power (and the Igbo agree they have it) to make rain in the dry season and to drive rain away in the rainy season. The "science" of rain making can be acquired by anybody who can pay the fee and will respect the taboo. Throughout his operations, which may last about a week if his services are required at a big second-burial ceremony, the rain maker may not take his bath or drink water. I have known of very successful and reputable rain makers. I have been to many Christian wedding feasts which were ruined because the services of the village rain maker were not employed. There are unsuccessful rain makers, of course, but they do not practice for long.

The operations of the rain makers are subject to the control of the community. They are not allowed to abuse their power. When the rain maker in my village attempted to abuse his power by "causing" much drought, my villagers resisted him and he was forced to abandon his profession altogether. He swore on *ɔfɔ* never to practice again in his lifetime. This was about six years ago. However, he sold his knowledge to his senior brother, who today operates within legitimate boundaries and has taught his eleven-year-old son the "science." This young rain maker, who is still in grade school, practices in the absence of his father. The fact that he is able to respect all the taboos suggests that they are not very burdensome.

In pre-British days, *Igwɛ* was developed into a big oracle, which had its center at Umunoha in Owerri. It was from Umunoha that neighboring communities bought the right to establish their own *igwɛ* shrines. These shrines were not competitive with but complementary to the all-powerful parent oracle at Umunoha. Like other oracles, the *igwɛ* of Umunoha also functioned as a final Court of appeal.

Since rivers in Igbo country are the subject of great veneration, it is Igbo belief that a big river has a "spiritual" principle which animates it. In some communities, it is forbidden to fish in such deified rivers or streams. This is a source of great conflict between those communities which uphold the "sacredness" of the fish in their streams and other Igbo and non-Igbo communities which show no respect for them. Among the southern Igbo communities on both sides of the Imo River, *imo miri* (*Imo* deity) is highly respected. It gives rise to a communal rite in which people participate annually. The rite is held during the annual flood, which occurs between May and July. At this rite, the *imo miri* is requested to bring more favors—children, an increase in wealth, for example—and to protect her worshipers for the next season.

People may swear their innocence before an *imo miri* shrine. Those who swear falsely before it are said to be liable to drown in the river or to suffer from water-logging disease. People who die in this way are denied ground burial. Those who die by drowning (either by suicide or otherwise) are buried on the bank of the river. They are believed to be taken away by *imo miri* during her annual floods.

In addition to the important deities, Igbo believe in other spirits which may be either personal or impersonal, benevolent or wicked, according to the circumstances. Their goodwill can be kept by being treated well. Only the wicked need fear them. Among the principal spirits are *agbara* or *alɘsi*. Forests and rivers lying in the fringes of cultivated land are said to be occupied by these spirits. The roles attributed to *agbara* are always bad. They are conceived as malicious spirits capable of causing barrenness and death. Oaths are taken on *agbara,* and appeals to them are confined to those instances where human judicial processes fail to give satisfaction. Their reputation depends on the number of guilty persons who have died or have met with misfortune after swearing falsely by them. The most reputable *agbara* are those which have achieved oracular status.

Important personal spirits which are worthy of mention include *mbataku* (spirit of wealth) and *aguɘ* (*agwɘ ishi, agwɘ nshi*). *Mbataku* is a ram-headed spirit to whom Igbo attribute their wealth. Before setting out on a journey, it is the usual Igbo practice to make a sacrifice to *mbataku*, perhaps only a piece of kola nut. If the journey proves successful, *mbataku* receives its reward. When trading faces a slump, *mbataku* is requested to provide better economic opportunities. If an animal strays into a compound and efforts to locate the owner fail, the animal is killed on the *mbataku* shrine, the "spirit of wealth" claiming the blood, while men feast on the carcass.

While the Igbo attitude toward their *mbataku* is that of identification, they exhibit much ambivalence toward *agwɘ ishi* (head spirit). They discuss *agwɘ* with horror and refer to it as *Onyɛ ukwu-a* ("The Big One"). The only Igbo willing to discuss *agwɘ* extensively are its servitors, who talk of their early horrible encounter with *agwɘ,* their long struggle to avoid it, and how they finally agreed to serve it.

Agwɘ is a most proselytizing spirit always in need of servitors. It is very envious of people's wealth, which paradoxically, it claims to bring. To serve *agwɘ* is to enter the long rites of ordination which may eventually make one a *dibia*. Not many people have the wealth and patience to attain this height. Some stop after the initial rites or at any stage of the ordination process where they feel they can confidently challenge *agwɘ* to provide the economic resources necessary to complete the rites. But to refuse *agwɘ's* call to its service is to face a long trial and temptation, involving loss of property, loss of children, barrenness, and, in many cases, *ara agwɘ,* psychosomatic syndromes. The effective weapon with which to combat *ara agwɘ* is performance of *igwɔ aja—* rites of priestly ordination.

Other important but less potentially harmful spirits include *aha njɔku* (*ifɛ jɔku*) (the yam spirit) and *ikoro* (the drum spirit). The ɛzɛ *ji* (yam chiefs) invoke *aha njɔku* during the yam title rites.

Aha Njɔku is a powerful spirit respected by the Igbo. Women call her *nwanyi dim*—a co-wife. She acts as a social sanction which controls the behavior of women in the home, the farm, and the *ɔba*—a storage place for yams. Women are obliged not to throw away yams in anger, an act that offends *aha njɔku*. But if they do and subsequently eat yams without appeasing *aha njɔku*, it is believed they will have dysentery or cholera. Out of respect for the yam spirit, fighting is not allowed on the farm. Quarreling on the farm must be appeased, and an egg is usually broken on the spot to ask for forgiveness.

Aha Njɔku brings "yam-oriented" children of both sexes called *Njɔku* (*Agbara-ji, Nwosu, Ifejɔku*) and *Mmaji*. It is the privilege of yam chiefs (*ɛzɛji*) to sire these children, a privilege that has proved a ritual burden in recent years. As the human representatives of the yam spirit, *Njɔku* and *Mmaji* are entitled to privileges. They have the right to any yam they may demand from the *ɔba*. This is a source of friction and envy between them and other less-privileged children. A *Njɔku* must marry an *Mmaji*. A *Mmaji* must be the first wife of her husband as well as the only wife with her ascribed status. Other co-wives must not be *Mmaji*. This type of prescribed status-linked marriage still persists even among literate Christians who happen to be *Njɔku* and *Mmaji*. At their deaths, the heads of *Njɔku* and *Mmaji* may not touch the ground. At burial, there is a raised platform to which a solid receiver is attached (an iron pot is now used) in order to collect the head as it falls off after decay. The head is then ritually dug out, washed, and put away in a box, which is placed on a raised platform built for the purpose.

Because of the havoc the improper care of these heads has been alleged to have caused some Igbo, they have developed an ambivalent attitude towards *Njɔku* or *Mmaji*. They are loved as status objects but hated for the problems they create at death, which automatically puts a taboo on yams. No member of the family may eat yam until the heads are ritually buried, a very costly affair.

Yam is a crop around which much of the social and religious life of Igbo center. Within each agricultural cycle every farmer offers about three sacrifices to *aha njɔku:* the beginning of the farming season (bush clearing or the first planting), the first harvest, and the final harvest. Devout priests do not eat "new" yam until a formal sacrifice is made to *aha njɔku*. The biggest communal rite is known as *irɔ ɔfɔ* or *ɔfala*. It is a thanksgiving ceremony in which the whole community participates. Each community holds the rite on its market day, when elaborate preparations for it are made. Women prepare food and oil beans, children fetch water and wood, and everyone else works to clear the village paths and the marketplace.

Very early on the appointed day, the village is alerted by the sounds of *ɔdɵ agwu*—the ivory horns used by priests. Rams, sheep, and chickens are slaughtered by compound and household heads, *aha njɔku* receiving the blood in a portable altar known as *ɛgbɔ aha njɔku*. At about ten in the morning the communal meal prepared at *ovu* (*obu*)—a reception hut—is ready. Children are given yams dipped in fresh palm oil. They are asked to take a bite of the yam, and to drop some crumbs as they run along the village paths. They are enjoined not to look behind for fear of scaring the spirits. As a child, this was a ritual activity I enjoyed most. It involved running, competitive eating, and dropping crumbs of yams along the trails. The eating, drinking, and feasting of guests used to last about four days.

Irɔ ɔfɔ provides an occasion for women who have had children during the year to give thanks: those who have had male children present cocks, and those who have had female children present hens.

Less important in Igbo life today than it was in pre-European days is *ikoro*—the drum deity. *Ikoro* represents the power of the community to make successful wars. The drum, which has a carved human head, is fashioned from a single block of wood and may be as high as six feet and as long as nine feet. Its human head is said to symbolize the maker, who is alleged to have been killed to "doctor" and vitalize the drum. It is drummed to mark a great occasion. Today *ikoro* remains symbolic of a glorious if warlike past. Its peacetime role occurs in important festivals, when it is drummed to communicate to the people the news of a great event (Uchendu 1964a: 32–33).

Other spirits include *ɛkwu*—the hearth spirit, which is women's domestic spirit. Children who neglect their aged mothers are cursed on the *ɛkwu*. During an epidemic of smallpox, *ɔgan' ɛlu*—the smallpox spirit—becomes important. Its human representative is thought to be an ugly old woman who is believed to hover about very early in the morning transmitting the disease by weaving cobwebs. Hence it is believed that traveling early in the morning exposes one to the danger of being entangled in the smallpox webs.

Igbo Oracles

Frequent references have been made to the Igbo oracles—the *agbara* of Awka, the *igwɛ* of Umunoha, the *kamalu* of Ɔzuzu, and the *ibini ɔkpabɛ* of Aro Chukwu (the "Long Juju")—and to their judicial role as the final court of appeal in Igboland. They have another important role, however, in the links they forge among many communities in Igboland.

The common characteristics of the Igbo oracles are their secret operations, the institutionalization of an "intelligence service" and the attraction of clients through a chain of contact agents. Their geographical locations indicate a regional influence or sphere of authority. But in the nineteenth century the "Long Juju" attained a position of supremacy over the others and was recognized as the most influential Igbo oracle. Nevertheless, the oracles were competitive and their Igbo clients could choose which one to consult. Where the oracular verdict contradicted the popular opinion, much doubt of its veracity was expressed, though little else could be done because of the prohibitive cost of "consulting" another oracle. The oracular verdict seemed to confirm popular opinions and prejudices and to shift the burden of making a difficult but necessary decision from the human to the spiritual domain.

The reputation of an oracle depended on the quality of its intelligence service. The "intelligence" officials were men who had much contact in those areas where their oracle was most influential. They were most knowledgeable about local and "foreign" affairs, and had means of investigating doubtful cases. Their "feel" for local opinion and prejudices was nearly perfect. Since clients must be "sponsored," it was not difficult to ascertain, through the relays of sponsors or contact agents, what the problem was. But the necessity to ascertain the facts caused long delays, and a journey which would normally take two days on foot might take weeks.

The Aro "Long Juju" had a most successful intelligence service, conducted by knowledgeable Aro at "home" and "abroad" (Aro had settlements in other Igbo communities). The fact that they did not trust such work to non-Aro explains why the oracular secrecy was maintained for so long.

Consulting an oracle is not simple or inexpensive. An informant who was impoverished by "going to *Igwɛ*" put the matter this way:

People who do not know my past cannot understand why I am like this [poor].

Many years ago, before I married the mother of *Uka* (about the late nineteenth century), people in my compound were dying like flies. Our local *dibia* and diviners could not stop the premature deaths. I decided to "go to *Igwɛ*," a journey that cost me the equivalent of "twenty head of women" [in terms of the then prevailing bridewealth payment] and took me to many towns. No one person knew the "road" to *Igwɛ*. You must pass "from hand to hand." You must consult a diviner with each change of escort to ascertain the auspiciousness of your journey. You must come back through the home of your escorts. Each escort had his price, the amount often settled by the oracle. Our journey took three weeks. Though I am a *dibia,* I could not help shivering when I heard the big voice of *Igwɛ.* The whole premises trembled when he appeared. He called my name, my father's and mother's names, as well as the name of my town. He named one after another the six young men and women who had died in my compound in less than two years. He demanded his price, an equivalent of "ten head of women," which I paid on the spot. [There is no "down payment."] He then told me "my story," the cause of the premature deaths. "An enemy had buried the head of a premature baby in my compound." This is the cause of the deaths, the *Igwɛ* confided. He recommended a *dibia* who would unearth the "premature" skull and specified his fee. This was done and "premature deaths" stopped.

I owe much to friends from *Ɔkpofɛ* [village in Mbaise]. I call them *ndi umunɛ-m*—my mother's natal home [because of the *umunɛ*-like role they played]. Going to *Igwɛ* is a big lesson. It helps. But it has left me [poor].

The number of Igbo deities, spirits, and oracles is enormous. Their anthropomorphous character is well recognized. The Igbo attitude toward the gods is not one of fear but one of friendship, a friendship that lasts as long as the reciprocal obligations are kept. This contractual quality in the man-spirit relationship is based on the recognition of the inadequacy of either party. Only the high god is self-sufficient. Nowhere is the contractual relationship between man and spirit better illustrated than in the Igbo attitude toward the ancestors.

The Ancestors

Ancestors occupy a special place in Igbo religious practice. The Igbo conceive of their ancestors as the invisible segment of the lineage. The ancestors are "honored" and not "worshiped" in the strict sense. The ancestral honor is a religion based on reciprocity. There is a loving reverence for the deceased ancestors, who are expected to come back to reincarnate and "do to the living members what they did for them."

Ancestors are scolded as if they were still living. This can be noticed in any sacrifice. They are reprimanded for failing in their duty to their children, by closing their eyes to the depredations of evil spirits which cause death in the family, cause crop failure, and make trade unprofitable. No elaborate sacrifices are made to ancestors. They are given the ordinary foods eaten in the home: water, raphia wine, and a piece of kola may be all.

The Igbo idea that the ancestors and other deceased members come back to "temporal life" is rooted in their theory of reincarnation. Belief in reincarnation gives the Igbo hope of realizing their frustrated status goals in the next cycle of life. Transmigration, on the other hand, is regarded as the greatest possible punishment for the incestuous, the murderer, the witch, and the sorcerer. *"Ilɔdigh uwa na mmadu"* "May you not reincarnate in the human form"—is a great curse for the Igbo. The reincarnation of those who violated taboos is usually said to be inauspicious. They are born either feet first or with teeth or as members of a twin set—all of which are in themselves taboo.

Although death of old age is accepted as a blessing by general consent, and death in childhood or youth, and death through accident is regarded as a tragedy, some Igbo reincarnate as *ɔgbanjɛ*—repeater. The *ɔgbanjɛ* die prematurely without any sign of ill-health. They can, however, be "stabilized" by specialist doctors, provided they can be detected in time.

Sacrifice is an integral part of Igbo religious practice. Igbo seek the divine will through oracles and divination. Revelation must be followed by some form of sacrifice, which may involve the whole political community, a lineage, a compound, or a family. Some sacrifices are obligatory (those recommended by the diviner) and others may be routine. Whatever their form, sacrifices show gratitude to the gods for past blessings, express hope for future favors, and request protection against all evils from wicked men and malignant spirits.

Igbo religious beliefs and practices are complex. They are based on the conception of a high god who has subordinate but "free" spirits, on the reincarnation doctrine which rationalizes people's status, and on the ancestors who protect the living from the wicked spirits. The revelation of divine will, which is ascertained through divination and oracular opinion, must be followed by sacrifice.

12

The Igbo and Culture Contact

THE PRECEDING OUTLINE of Igbo culture may be briefly summarized. The Igbo lay a great emphasis on individual achievement and initiative. There are no restraints, human, cultural, or supernatural, which cannot, theoretically, be overcome. The individual's "bargain" for his status goal begins with ɛbibi and continues through reincarnation, when a soul makes a choice which determines his "fate," a fate which he is able to "manipulate" to his relative advantage if things do not go well for him on earth. Related to the individual's "role bargaining" is an interest in long-range goals, the manipulation of supernatural power to augment one's self-power, and the symbolic acquisition of personal power through eating the "heart" of brave enemies.

Igbo individualism is not "rugged" individualism; it is individualism rooted in group solidarity. The Igbo realize that "a river does not eat a blind calabash" (that is, a person with backers escapes dangers unhurt). There is a great emphasis on communal cooperation and achievement. The "communal" character of the Igbo must be traced to the formative influence of their traditional social patterns, the influence of their nucleated residence pattern, and the ideological urge "to get up." The ideal of cooperation, illustrated in work groups, credit associations, and title-making societies, pervades all aspects of Igbo culture.

The society offers alternative prestige goals and paths to fame. The traditional government is a direct democracy in which leadership is achieved on a competitive basis. The priesthood, farming, title societies, warfare, and trading are among the traditional avenues to status. These occupations are not hierarchically ranked and distinction in one field is as good as in another.

The political system is conciliar and competitive. Leadership is democratic in character, and the village government gives much latitude to the youth. It is *ability* rather than *age* that qualifies for leadership.

Igboland is unevenly populated, and many areas are experiencing a population pressure. This has led to many "secondary" migrations within Igboland and a consequent resettlement of minorities in many parts of it. However, cultural borrowings and cultural integration had been going on centuries before the European intrusion.

The bearers of Igbo culture have been most willing to accept the changes resulting from European contact. Land hunger and population pressure are always among the many reasons given for Igbo receptivity to change. In a paper devoted to this question, Ottenberg discusses these four factors: the influence of the European slave trade on the Igbo, the nature of direct European contact following the slave trade, the nature and organization of Igbo culture, and the high population density in Igbo country (1962:132–143). But an important ideological factor is omitted: the Igbo ideas about change. A people who fear change and are ideologically opposed to experimentation might not react in the same way (assuming similar contact situations) as do people who believe that change is part of the established order. The Igbo believe that change is necessary for the realization of their long-term goals. Whatever improves the individual's and community's status is acceptable to the Igbo. This is the key to their attitude toward innovation.

The Igbo were involved in both the slave-trade operations of the seventeenth and nineteenth centuries and the palm-produce trade which superseded it. They were at one time slavers or slaves, and then agents to the middlemen who dealt in palm produce. The cultural impact of the slave trade on the Igbo was the rise to a position of supremacy of the Aro oracle known as the "Long Juju," as well as possible social and demographic changes in the slaving areas. It was at this time that a major Igbo staple, cassava (manioc), came from the New World. Other trade "currencies," such as whisky (*Wishikiri,* Igbo), guns, and gunpowder, were introduced and soon became part of the Igbo culture complex.

When Britain attempted to take over political control of Igboland in the early decades of this century, there were resistances and cultural protests. A nativistic religious movement, the *ɛkumeku,* which sprang up, inspired short-lived but feverish messianic enthusiasm. The rumor that Igbo women were being assessed for taxation sparked off the 1929 Aba Riots, a massive revolt of women never before encountered in Igbo history.

When the Igbo became reconciled to their political fate they lost no time in exploiting the economic opportunities offered by better roads, wider markets, and opportunity to buy machine-made goods through earnings from paid labor and export produce. With the growth of cities, many a rural-based Igbo has become a city dweller. Through the Family Meetings and Improvement Unions, he maintains his solidarity with his natal village, contributes to its welfare programs, and shapes its opinion on social and political questions. A "detribalized" or "marginal" Igbo who walks in the corridor between two cultures and belongs to neither is yet to be found. This is not due to any unique quality of the Igbo; rather, it is due to the nature of the Igbo contact situation. There is no "white settler" problem. What white population there is, lives in the city, except for the occasional missionary or the district officers, who live on a "reservation." The contact situation has not greatly disturbed the continuity of social patterns and cultural transmission among the Igbo. Socialization of children is still shared by the village and the city and interaction in many city affairs is based on kinship cues.

Innovations among the Igbo are self-sponsored. For instance, the missionaries "opened" schools and still "manage" them, but the Igbo built them and own them. The schools are their property, status symbols. It is in the same spirit that colleges, maternity centers, hospitals, and wells are built. They are all a part of the community effort, a demonstration of community achievement; a way of making the community "get up."

The Igbo, an increasingly mobile people in recent years, are found in all major Nigerian cities. Many seek paid labor in agricultural fields outside Nigeria, such as the Cameroons, Fernando Póo, and Río Muni. They are willing to do any type of work. Because of this they are held in contempt by some of their neighbors who paradoxically refer to the Igbo as a model of a hard-working, "go-ahead" people, thus creating a sort of ambivalent attitude toward Igbo: a hard-working people but people who are willing to do demeaning work. But the Igbo are well represented in all occupations in Nigeria, ranging from the highest to the lowest.

The mobility of the Igbo has been explained by land hunger, the poverty of the soil of Igboland, and the high population density. These factors are no doubt correlated with Igbo mobility, but physical mobility is not a recent phenomenon for this restless people. Nor is population pressure general. The areas of high population density are also the areas of poor soil as well as the areas of greatest missionary activity and educational opportunity. Educated Igbo, as is true of most educated Africans, earn their living in the city, where their skills are demanded. But why the Igbo are so mobile cannot be solely explained by land hunger, though it is a great factor. The matter of differential earnings from land and paid labor must be considered. Igbo agriculture is very primitive in comparison with other Igbo developments. It is still a hoe culture; farming for prestige rather than for profit is its basis. The "flight" from the land to the city is not due to any disdain for agriculture as such; rather, it is a rational economic decision and shows a preference for a system which promises better tangible rewards.

In a contact situation, people tend to select those cultural traits which can be easily reconciled with their own existing cultural pattern. The more freedom of choice a receiving culture has, the greater its degree of selectivity. This is true of the Igbo case and helps to explain the apparent paradox that "of all Nigerian peoples, the Ibo have probably changed the least while changing the most" (Ottenberg 1962: 142). The nature of the contact situation has made it possible for the Igbo to accept certain innovations, modify certain elements of their social, religious, economic, and political structure in order to accommodate the changes, and retain other basic patterns, such as achievement-orientation, long-term goals, hatred of autocracy, and a strong communal character.

Igbo receptivity to change is explained by their ideal of progress as expressed in their concept of "getting up," the flexibility of their social structure, the cooperative yet competitive character which makes adjustment in the city easy, the nature of the contact situation in which they were not "overwhelmed," the long period of Euro-Igbo contact which developed trading partnerships collaboration while it introduced new "wants"—all this before the period of political domination and the relative impoverishment of the land by the demands of a growing population.

Orthography

A few words must be said about the orthography used. For most words, I have used what is called the "new" orthography while retaining the old spellings for cities and village-groups as they appear in maps and official documents.

The Igbo Alphabet

a	b	c	d	e	ɛ	f	g	gb	gh	h	i
j	k	kp	l	m	n	ŋ	o	ɔ	ɵ	p	ɾ
s	t	u	v	w	y	z	gw	kw	nw	ny	

The consonants have approximately the values they have in English: b, c (as in *church*), d, f, g, gb, gh, h, j, k, kp, l, m, n, ŋ (as in *sing*), p, ɾ, s, t, v, w, y, z, gw, kw (as in *quit*), nw, ny.

The following values are assigned to the vowels:

Symbol	English equivalent	Igbo
a	fat	ala
e	sit	eta
i	meet	ji
ɛ	ten	ɛzɛ
o	note	obi
u	food	ubɛ
ɔ	oil	ɔfɔ
ɵ	mug	ɵmɵ

References

ARDENER, E. W., 1954, "The Kinship Terminology of a Group of Southern Ibo," *Africa,* Vol. 24, No. 2, pp. 85–99.

ARDENER, S. G., 1953, "The Social and Economic Significance of the Contribution Club among a Section of the Southern Ibo," Annual Conference, Sociology Section, Ibadan, March, 1953, West African Institute of Social and Economic Research, Ibadan, Nigeria, University College, pp. 128–142.

BASDEN, G. T., 1921, *Among the Ibos of Southern Nigeria.* London: Seeley Service.

————, 1938, *Niger Ibos.* London: Seeley Service.

DIKE, K. O., 1956, *Trade and Politics in the Niger Delta* (1830–1885). Oxford: Clarendon Press.

GREEN, M. M., 1947, *Ibo Village Affairs.* London: Sidgwick & Jackson, Ltd.

GREENBERG, J. H., 1949, "Studies in African Linguistic Classification: The Niger-Congo Family," *Southwestern Journal of Anthropology,* Vol. 5, No. 2, pp. 79–100.

HERSKOVITS, M. J., 1931, *Life in a Haitian Valley.* New York: Alfred A. Knopf, Inc.

HORTON, W. R. G., 1954, "The *Ohu* System of Slavery in a Northern Ibo Village-Group," *Africa,* Vol. 24, pp. 311–336.

JONES, G. I., 1956, *The "Jones Report": Report on the Status of Chiefs,* Eastern Nigeria, Enugu, Nigeria, Government Printer.

JORDAN, J. P., 1949, *Bishop Shanahan of Southern Nigeria.* Dublin: Clonmore & Reynolds.

LEITH-ROSS, S., 1937, "Notes on the *Osu* System among the Ibo of Owerri Province, Nigeria," *Africa,* Vol. 10, pp. 206–220.

NWABUEZE, B. O., 1963, *The Machinery of Justice in Nigeria,* London, Butterworth & Co. (Publishers), Ltd.

OTTENBERG, S., 1958, "Ibo Oracles and Inter-group relations," *Southwestern Journal of Anthropology,* Vol. 14, pp. 294–317.

————, 1962, "Ibo Receptivity to Change," *Continuity and Change in African Cultures,* W. J. Bascom and M. J. Herskovits (eds.). Chicago: University of Chicago Press, Phoenix Edition, pp. 130–143.

PERHAM, M., 1962, *Native Administration in Nigeria*, London: Oxford University Press.

UCHENDU, V. C., 1963, "Status and Hierarchy among the Southeastern Igbo," unpublished Master's thesis, Northwestern University, Evanston, Ill.

———, 1964a, "The Status Implications of Igbo Religious Beliefs." *The Nigerian Field*, Vol. 29, No. 1, pp. 27–37.

———, 1964b, "Kola Hospitality and Igbo Lineage Structure," *Man*, No. 53, pp. 47–50.

WIESCHHOFF, H. A., 1941, "Social Significance of Names among the Ibo of Nigeria," *American Anthropologist*, Vol. 43, pp. 212–222.

Recommended Reading

BASDEN, G. T., 1921, *Among the Ibos of Southern Nigeria*. London: Seeley Service.

———, 1938, *Niger Ibos*. London: Seeley Service.

These two books complement each other. Written by a missionary who knew his Igbo, they provide a general ethnographic picture of the Onitsha-Awka hinterland in the early decades of this century.

FORDE, D., and G. I. JONES, 1950, *The Ibo and Ibibio-Speaking Peoples of South-eastern Nigeria,* London: International African Institute.

Provides a broad ethnographic survey of Igbo culture. Attempts a culture area division of Igbo and maps major Igbo social groupings. Includes an extensive ethnographic bibliography and a good map.

GREEN, M. M., 1947, *Ibo Village Affairs*. London: Sidgwick & Jackson, Ltd.

By no means a well-rounded village study, this book, nevertheless, presents a clear picture of women's activities in Agbaja village-group, Okigwi District. The theories of Igbo temperament presented by the author (an afterthought) do not appear as convincing as her brilliant functional analysis of this social system. This is the only available village study on Igbo by a professional anthropologist.

MEEK, C. K., 1937, *Law and Authority in a Nigerian Tribe,* London: Oxford University Press, 1937.

This authoritative study of the Igbo sociopolitical system contains comparative areal data and an analysis of Igbo authority patterns.

NZEKWU, ONUORA, 1963, *Wand of Noble Wood,* New York: New American Library of World Literature, Inc., Signet Edition (paperback).

An interesting novel by an Igbo depicting the sociocultural conflicts and tensions in present-day Igbo society. The problems of *diala-osu* marriage, the fatality of the Igbo "curse way," the power of the oracles, and the conflicting obligations of the Igbo educated elite are all presented in this little novel.